School Daze & Beyond

To my Dear cousin Keith & Family
Hope that this book fills in some of
the gaps and brings back pleasant
memories of yesteryear.

Veeshti·
July 7, 2009

School Daze & Beyond

Vashti Hinds

iUniverse, Inc.
New York Bloomington

School Daze & Beyond

Copyright © 2008 by Vashti Hinds

iUniverse books may be ordered through booksellers or by contacting:

iUniverse
1663 Liberty Drive
Bloomington, IN 47403
www.iuniverse.com
1-800-Authors (1-800-288-4677)

ISBN: 978-0-595-52088-6 (pbk)
ISBN: 978-0-595-62154-5 (ebk)

Printed in the United States of America

iUniverse rev. date: 4/22/2009

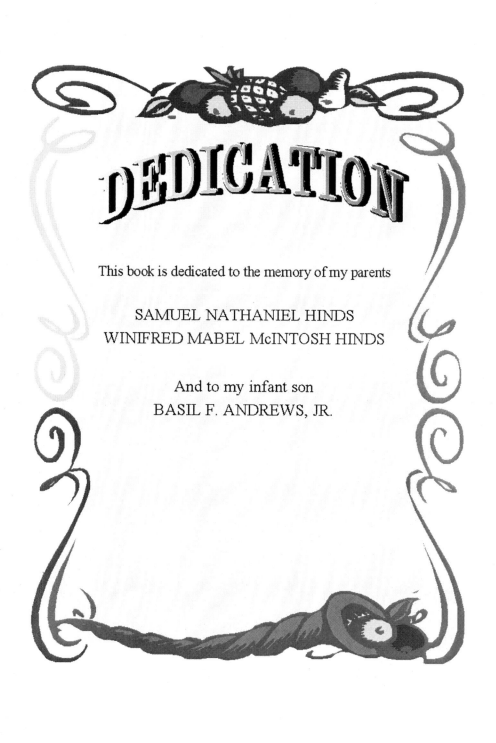

DEDICATION

This book is dedicated to the memory of my parents

SAMUEL NATHANIEL HINDS
WINIFRED MABEL McINTOSH HINDS

And to my infant son
BASIL F. ANDREWS, JR.

ACKNOWLEDGEMENTS

First, I acknowledge the goodness of God who inspired me to write this book, supplying the motivation and focus so that this entire book was hand written in less than three weeks. I acknowledge the contributions of my elementary School Teachers Mavis Carr-Thompson, Clarene Nelson-Williams, Clement Jones, Hector Paris and my headmasters Mr. McGowan and Mr. Marshall. The support of the Silver Set of the McIntosh family was invaluable - Connie, Daphne, Jean, Ingrid and Ezme - also Wilfred David and Carmen Barclay Subryan for corroborating some dates and events mentioned in the book. My brother David Hinds has always encouraged me to write. I thank him and his children Imari and Bakara for their support. My son Sheldon K. Andrews has contributed his skill as a Graphic Artist, supplying all the illustrations, my daughter-in-law Anita is recognized for her technical assistance on the computer. My niece Abina Wood has sacrificed her time, though employed full time and at the same time completing a Master Degree to type most of the manuscript. I owe a debt of gratitude to Lily Bernard-Burchett and Iris Catticart-Harewood (recently deceased) who stepped in to bridge the gap when I lost my mother. My life long friends Flora Dublin, Paula Allicock, Grace Cush-Elliott, Phyllis Dyer-Meridin, Rosetta Ryan-Allyne, Dr. Millicent Francis-Lane, Yvonne Andrews-Artis, Semoy Cipriani, Celeste Abraham, Deslyn Fordice, Othniel Saul, Carlyle Skinner, Anne Fridal, members of the Hinds family, Bernice Johnson and a host of others who significantly contributed to the success of the book whether they were aware of it or not. Special thanks to Jerry Cox for revisiting the tune to the Alphabet Song. I am also indebted to my nursing colleagues in Trinidad, New York and North Carolina, bearing in mind that all experiences in life whether good or bad have contributed to this finished product. Thanks to all of you!

INTRODUCTION

This book started out primarily as a children's story book, documenting stories told to me by my mother, followed by my own true life stories from which, later in life, I drew many spiritual conclusions and comparisons. I was reluctant to let them go undocumented as they held for me such meaning and pleasant memories.

As I progressed in recounting the incidents, which are all true, I was obliged to include some historical facts and physical settings in British Guiana as a backdrop to the stories. In retrospect, being raised by the whole community in a British Colony, knowing that the discipline enforced by the elders was engendered by love in an effort to pass on to us the best they knew makes us aware that our heritage is rich indeed. On the walls of the Methodist School in Friendship Village this verse, which was clearly visible to all students, captured the sentiments of the teachers and village elders as they encouraged us to reach for the stars:

Good, Better, Best
Never let it rest,
Until your good is better
And your better, best.

ANON

It also seemed natural for me to write about what I knew best - my family. The writing for me was effortless as the information simply flowed freely. I hope that this book reawakens some of the precious memories of yesteryear, and also allows the next generation a peek into the past, dispelling the myth that we led boring lives before the advent of television and video games.

Happy Reading.

Contents

Freight Car Harry

Reference Texts
Ex. 20:12
Eph. 6:2

Boys and girls, this is a true story told to me by my mother which took place approximately in 1925. There was a boy in her class named Harry who was often teased for being obedient to his father who was a single parent . Harry's father was also the village shoemaker and the agent for the Evening News. Harry headed for home right after school to do his chores and to help his father in distributing the newspapers and returning shoes that had been repaired to customers.

"Harry, there are some ripe mangoes on Mr. Kirby's tree" Kenny said, with excitement dancing in his eyes. "The boys are going to get their share after school. Want to come along?"

"Sorry, Kenny, but you know I can't. I have to help my father at home and besides, it is not right to steal."

"What did I tell you?" Leland chimed in. "He is too perfect to have a little fun. He always has to obey his father. He will never have fun like us. Don't ever ask him again."

Harry hurried home and at supper he confided to his father how he felt at being teased. His father understood but quoted the scripture about honoring par-ents for which God promises a long life. His father said "Har-ry I want you to have fun and time for that will come, but prom-ise me that whenever or wherever you hear my voice, you will obey." Harry prom-

ised and fell asleep, happy because the next day was a holiday from school and he would not have to listen to the teasings from the boys.

Two passenger trains passed through the village every day: one going to the town early in the morning and one coming from the town in the evening. The trains were pulled by great big steam engines which puffed billows of black smoke which had a peculiar but heavenly smell as the engine chugged, chugged along. Some time before lunch a freight train passed through with supplies for the grocers and other businesses in their box cars. Harry's family lived right near the train station. People usually walked along the tracks (no 3rd rail) when trains were not expected.

After breakfast and morning chores, Harry's father said to him "Harry, I want you to take these shoes to Mrs. Rodney. Tell her they cost two bits for the repair."

"Right away, dad. Do you think I could walk on the tracks? It would be a short cut. I would be back in no time at all."

"I reckon so. The freight train has already passed, but do be careful" his dad cautioned.

Harry started out whistling a tune as soon as he got out of earshot of his father (in those days children did not whistle in the presence of grown ups; it was thought to be rude). His father returned to his work, but suddenly he had a feeling that made him uneasy, so he went to the veranda to see how far Harry had gotten to and what he saw made his heart come up to his throat (meaning, he froze).

Immediately he screamed "Harry, lie down flat right now!"

Being obedient Harry did as he was told without a moment's hesitation or looking around to see who was looking at him lying on the tracks. He was taught to obey and that he did. No sooner had he obeyed a freight car rolled over him and he, in turn, froze where he was until his father told him that it was all right to get up.

The last car from the freight train had somehow become dislodged from the rest of the train and had silently rolled back (down a slight decline) without warning. The engineer was unaware of this and was therefore unable to blow the distress whistle to warn the villagers of the danger. Had Harry not obeyed his father promptly, he would have been killed by the box car from the freight train which was very well laden with merchandise.

What a lesson and testimony that was to the boys at his school particularly! Boys and girls, the Bible says that if we honor our parents, our days will be long upon the land which the Lord our God gives us. Of all the Commandments, this is the first one which carries a promise. God was therefore thinking of you, letting you know that He desires you to live a long life. Let us all be obedient to our parents, honoring them every way we can.

"HAPPY BIRTHDAY TO YOU"

Reference Texts
Hos 8:7
Matt. 7:12

This story about a wicked king was told to me by my mother. It seemed that there was a poor man who begged for alms (food and money) everyday at the palace gate as he chanted his mantra-"Do good, and good will follow you; do bad and bad will follow you".

It annoyed the king to hear this off scale song every time he went in and out of the palace gates on his way to and from his royal functions and ceremonies. Many attempts were made to remove the man to another location but he inevitably found his way right back to the palace gates. Several dignitaries had also complained to the king of what a nuisance the man was becoming with this song and his unkempt attire. The king decided that he would have to get rid of this man once and for all.

Calling to his chief butler, the king said "I want you to make the nicest cake for the old begger."

"Do you mean it?" the butler asked in surprise.

"Sure I do!" replied the king, with a twinkle in his eyes, " I want this to be the best cake he ever ate, so much so that it will be his last," then adding "Do what you have to do."

Anxious to gain favor with the king, the butler baked the cake and decorated it with strawberry frosting, sprinkles, even putting candles on the cake. Oh! I forgot to mention that the butler added a towering tablespoon of Arsenic to the frosting. The butler put the cake in a pretty box with a bow and ribbons on it, and brought it out to the beggar.

"How did the king know that it was your birthday?" he said as he approached the beggar.

Surprised, the beggar denied that it was his birthday. The butler pressed on "Are you sure? Well, just enjoy this gorgeous cake that he commissioned me to make for you. Enjoy it in good health."

The beggar accepted the box, saying as he did so "Thank you good man and thank the king heartily for me. It's as I always say "do good and good will follow you, do bad and bad will follow you. Long life and blessings to the king and his family. God save the king!"

The beggar was excited to have the cake, but he decided to hurry home to his hut in the forest to eat his cake without interruptions. He was just about to begin eating when he heard the sound of a horse's hooves. He hobbled to the door in time to see the crown prince alighting from his horse. The man bowed to the prince, asking "What brings you to my humble abode so late in the evening, my Lord Prince?" "Today, I thought that I would go off by myself to do some hunting. I sometimes get tired of being followed around by the royal archers all the time, but I have been going

around in circles for a while now, and I'm embarrassed to admit that I'm lost. Do you know the way back to the palace? I've been out here for the greater part of the day and I'm beginning to get hungry", the prince explained.

"Did you say you were hungry? Well, what a coincidence. Your father the king had his butler bake me such a great cake

and it was not even my birthday. Please have it, please. I didn't think I deserved it, but it's what I always say, "do good and good will follow you, do bad and bad will follow you."

"When he sent me the cake, little did he know that his kind act would so soon be rewarded. I am happy to return the cake to you with my blessing." The beggar gave the box with the cake to the prince with directions to the palace and turned into bed, happy that he was able to return the favor to the king. The prince galloped off in the direction he was given, munching on the cake as he went. He began to feel weak and then there was also a stabbing pain in his stomach. "I guess I was much hungrier than I thought" mused the prince as he rode on.

Soon he was feeling very ill, but his spirit revived when he saw the gates of the palace in the distance. "If I could only make it to the gates, I'll have all the help I need. This pain is becoming more severe and it is even difficult to breathe without some effort. I wonder what's wrong with me?" the prince thought.

The prince slid off his horse as he approached the gates. The guards rushed up to him and saw that his color was deathly, he was sweating profusely and he was doubled over in pain. They rushed him into the palace and called the court physician. The king immediately dropped everything and ran into the prince's room in disbelief at the condition in when he found his son.

On hearing that the prince had been out hunting alone, he asked nervously "Did you eat any wild berries growing near the cave, son?"

"No father," the prince gasped, "the only thing I ate was a cake from the man who begs at our gate." Panting for breath, he continued, "I became lost and came upon him in his house." He squeezed his abdomen in extreme agony and continued "He gave me directions to the palace and when I mentioned that I was hungry, he gave me the cake you gave him. Wasn't that nice of him father?"

"Sure it was, son, it sure was nice of him," the king sadly shook his head. Within the hour the prince had died. The king could not be consoled. He would always remember: "do good and good will follow you, do bad and bad will follow you."

The Bible teaches us that we should only do to others what we would not mind being done to us because a person reaps what he sows. If we sow the wind, we can expect to reap the whirlwind. We also always reap more than we sow, so sow only seeds of kindness.

THE FLOOD THAT NEVER CAME

References:
Mal. 3:10 – 11

Hello girls and boys! Today our story (which is a true one) is based on Malachi 3:10 and 11. This is a portion of the scripture that you would do well to remember for the rest of your lives. I know that you have heard the pastor and other grown-ups talking about tithes and offerings and perhaps you felt left out because you don't yet have a job to give one-tenth of your earnings to the Lord, but even now consider yourselves to be rich. Jesus takes notice of your offerings especially when given with the right attitude as he did the widow's mite.

Verse 11 goes on to say that the Lord will rebuke the devourer for our sakes if we are faithful with our tithes and offerings. You may ask "What is a devourer?" Well, I'm glad you asked. A devourer is anything or anyone who takes from you anything you did not give them. The head devourer is the devil and he can cause fire, floods, loss of money or property or any such calamity to come against you as he did with Job.

Anyway, I was raised by a mother who was an ardent tither. There was a small drawer on the upper right side of the dresser which was designated as the "tithe drawer." Every night when my mother came home, she assessed her tithes from our business and put it into that drawer and everyone in the home knew that that drawer was off limits. You were not allowed to even look inside -- something like "The Most Holy Place."

When I was approximately 10 years old, we needed a new roof. My mother made the arrangements with the contractor to begin work the following Sunday morning. She was also expected to travel to the town to obtain merchandise for our business as she did every Sunday morning. It took a full day of travel to the town, one day to do business, and one day to travel back home. The crew arrived very early and began work before she left.

Rain fell almost every day even if only for a few minutes. It could rain very heavily without warning, causing minor flooding. In practically no time at all they had removed the old roof and of all the times, we looked up and the blackest storm clouds were gathering in the sky. Some neighbors came out and started to forecast doom, predicting that our house would be flooded since in those days the roofers did not have many tarps to cover everything securely. I looked at my mother with fear in my eyes because I knew that she would soon be leaving us alone to be the ridicule of the neighbors, should the rain really come.

In today's language you could say that my mother was "something else." She said with her hands akimbo, (that's with her hands on her hips) "Well, I'm a tither and God will just have to keep his word. He is doing His work, so let me do mine" and off she went. I can remember wanting to go and hide myself somewhere, but being the eldest, I tried to act as if I echoed her sentiments. We lived on the bank of a wide river, and for the sake of reference for my New York City kids, our house would be on the Manhattan side of the East River. The crew was working feverishly to escape the inevitable coming rain when, after about the space of half an hour, the rain started on the Brooklyn side of the river. All heads were now turned towards the big, fat drops as they sounded on the water and the neighbors started to scamper to their homes to watch the soaking and ensuing flooding of our house from a safe distance.

After the space of five minutes, without hearing any drops of rain on their galvanized zinc roofs, the neighbors and the workmen realized that something unusual was happening. You'll never guess! The rain had only come to the middle of the river and stopped as if God had said "Thus far and no further." I can't tell you what a relief that was to me. The neighbors were the first to let my mother know of our miracle when she

returned home. Some of them even gave offerings to my mother to put in the collection plate for them.

The "head devourer" (the devil) is always trying to tempt you to doubt God and come up with excuses for withholding your tithes and offerings. You cannot be too young for him to try to make you doubt God. When I was younger Pastor Bob's Uncle, Mr. Mounter, owned a "cakeshop" (candy store) conviently right next door to the church. I was tempted many times to make a quick run when my mother was not looking. He would not have sold me anything though because he knew that we were not supposed to shop on Sabbath. He would also have told my mother.

Girls and boys, you have lots of money given to you by relatives at Christmas and you are bound to get some more for your birthdays. In addition to what your parents give you for offerings, get in the habit of giving some of your own money without being told and watch God "rebuke the devourer for your sake." He is our "head rebuker."

THE BLACK PATENT LEATHER SHOES

Reference Texts
Num. 32:23

Hello again boys and girls! The lesson I learned from this story was "be sure your sins will find you out" taken from right there in Numbers 32:23.

I must have been about 3 years old because my father was still alive and my brother had not yet been born. Both of my parents were Literature Evangelists (at that time they were known as Colporteurs) who went from home to home to sell Bibles, and books like the *Desire of Ages, Steps to Christ* and *Patriarchs and Prophets*. One Sunday, our pastor and some church members planned to visit a sick member who lived 14 miles down river, of course by paddle boat. Since most people were usually at home on Sundays, my parents made good use of Sundays to promote sales or collect balances. It was decided that I would wait for the pastor at the neighbor's and go along for the boat ride. My heart was all set on it.

When the boat arrived, however, it was raining and some additional members decided at the last minute to make the visit; so Pastor Fred Morales decided that is was too risky to overload the boat. You guessed it-I was left behind. Needless to say, I was disappointed. When they left I pouted, and instead of returning to the neighbor's, I went to my home thinking of ways to vent my frustration. Then it occurred to me-why not put on the new black shiny patent leather shoes my parents had bought me for 13th Sabbath? I knew where they were, in the shoebox under the chest of drawers. After all, I was only going to put them on and replace them in the box. After walking around the house for a while I thought I should let Diana see them since she didn't believe that my parents had really bought me new shoes.

Backing up a bit, let me tell you about 13th Sabbath. Anybody who was anybody got a new outfit from hat to shoes, even the grown ups! Can you believe this? The children recited all 13 memory texts for the quarter and acted out little plays, sang and just impressed the grown ups. We looked really cute with our hair ribbons, purses, knitted socks, new dressers, hats and shoes. We were so restless in the children's

10

division until it was time to come out, that our teachers were relieved when it was all over.

So I thought that I would slip out to let Diana see my new shoes, and remember I said that it was raining and nothing likes rain like mud, especially in Guyana! I showed my shoes to Diana, to Norma, her sister and all the children in the neighborhood who were very impressed with its newness. When I thought that it was about time for my parents to return home, I took the shoes off and politely replaced them in the box and pushed the box back under the chest of drawers.

My parents were surprised to see me at home, so I told them everything-except my adventure with the shoes and since they did not see through me, as I feared, I thought that my secret was safe.

My father had built me a little box in place of a stage, taught me how to bow and to recite my poem.

Some say give me silver
Some say give me gold
But I say give me Jesus
To save my little soul.

Brother Hinds was going to be so proud this 13th Sabbath.

13th Sabbath morning dawned bright and fair and my father proudly pulled out the shoebox to dress his baby girl, suddenly a gasp escaped his lips on seeing the dried mud on the black patent leather shoes. He showed the shoes to me and I began to cry. He tried to console me, but my mother kept saying "She's not too young to learn, be sure your sins will find you out". Had it not been the Sabbath I would have been the recipient of you know what, from my mother. My Daddy could never really punish me without feeling it himself.

So boys and girls, sometimes it

seems as though no one takes notice of all the good you do, but just do that one wrong thing and everybody knows. But, always remember what King David said in Psalm 139:11, "If I say surely the darkness shall cover me; even the night shall be light about me". As sure as the night follows the day, "be sure your sins will find you out." God is always watching. He sees the good as well as the bad. But, if you are really sorry for the wrong things you do, He'll forgive you, just as my Daddy and eventually my Mom did.

P.S. My father was not destined to be proud of me that day at all. At church I ascended the stage, bowed and began my recitation. No sooner had I started the second line, I burst into tears. Samuel Hinds took two giant steps to the stage and gently took me up in his arms where I stayed for the remainder of the service.

"NICE TO FINALLY MEET YOU ALL"

Reference Texts:
Psalm 37:4
John 10:11

At age five I began my elementary school education at Christiansburg Church of Scotland School 65 miles up the Demerara River from the capitol, Georgetown. My first grade teacher lived next door so that when classes began that September my mother just sent me along with her - no registration, no ceremony, nothing. Most of the children were from the neighborhood or from my congregation, so I felt quite at home almost at once. My mother bought at least two slates (writing tablets) at a time expecting the inevitable breakage. We sharpened our pencils on the concrete steps and looked smart in our maroon uniforms.

In the same compound there were the Manse for the Minister's family, the church, with a bell at the right front of the church, and a big, round vat at the back of the church which collected rain water. Across the road from the school, at the riverside was a huge Mora tree, under the shade of which concerts were conducted by the Country's Militia Band which kept a regular schedule. We brought the school benches out under the tree to accommodate the grown ups who did not bring their own chairs.

When ever the resident minister was not an ordained member of clergy, the overseer of the church scheduled quarterly visits to the region to perform weddings, christen babies, administer Communion, and evaluate the school's performance. Any out of town dignitaries, such as ministers of any religion, the magistrate for monthly court session was housed at the Rest House which was a short distance from the school. On the Monday morning following, the whole assembly was hurried into the church for service instead of the usual morning hymn and prayer in the school. The little ones sat in the front pews, but it was still difficult to see the overseer on the high alter. The view was slightly better when he ascended up into the elevated pulpit for his discourse. He always started off by saying in a monotone heavy Scottish accent, "God is a spirit and they that worship him must worship Him in spirit and in truth. Let us pray."

Patterson's great house of the 1800s, which later became Christianburg Court House.

Photo credit: Special thanks to Paul Mueller
The building next to the Court House is the Sawmill as it was in the mid 1800's.

The old sawmill waterwheel which operated at Plantation Christianburg, is still there.

After the prayer he eventually came around to telling us about the sheep high up in the hills of Scotland. He went on and on about these sheep every time that subconsciously we found ourselves straining our necks and eyes to see these sheep. For weeks after his visit I could not get those sheep out of my mind. In fact, I worried about them. I wondered if they went home at night, if they ever got lost, did wolves catch them, did they all have names. As a small child I could not conceive the idea of flocks of sheep because I had only seen a few sheep at a time. If I encountered difficulty sleeping for any reason and anybody had suggested sheep counting, guess which sheep I counted? You guessed right!

Walking home from school we passed the Commisary Houses on the left, Mama and Papa Allicock's house on the right, while extricating beads from the road, which would later on be strung to make bracelets and necklaces. Next we passed the out houses for the Courthouse, guava trees, jamoon trees, lemon trees but getting past the Rest House was a real test of endurance. You see, there were these Malacca trees (Trinidad, Pomerac) outside the compound which bore the most succulent, dark red almost black, fruit, but inside the compound was this tree bearing "White Lady" species of guava. These were large, whitish guava with small seeds, more fleshy with hardly a worm. How we prayed that one would fall outside the fence! We dared not enter the compound unless summoned by the caretaker to take a message or run an errand and even though court was not always in session, there was no shouting or horse play. You passed the Rest House with respect. On court days the women were required to wear hats in the courtroom, men wore ties and jackets. We passed by in patient suffrage. If we happened to see any of the caretakers we had to be sure to say, "Good afternoon" or "Good morning" just loud enough for them to acknowledge.

The Rest House was originally called the John D. Paterson's Great House built by British Major J.D. Paterson soon after he bought the sugar plantation in 1810. JD Paterson soon realized that there would soon be a bigger market for lumber. Paterson built a sawmill, the first water propelled one in the colony, just past the Great House. Paterson, who came to the area later, was a friend of Robert Allicock who initially settled the area in the 1770's. He traveled from Scotland in the late 1760's. My friend, author of many books including "Black Water

People" in which the history of the area is recorded, is an 8th generation descendant of Robert F. Allicock. Her grandfather was our next door neighbor. The headstones of J.D. Paterson and family are still in the yard of the Rest House, also the cannons which were fired to call his friends over for parties.

The old sawmill now served as the undeclared battleground where disagreements which were nursed all week long, were settled. We only needed two lookouts, one in each direction, to alert the contestants, spectators and cheering section, of the approach of grown ups, whereupon we would hastily disperse. Passing the Rest House I wondered whether the sheep had enough to eat; I was enjoying all the guavas, jamoons, the whitey, star apples, mangoes and locust on the way home. I passed the Daisy mound (green sweet smelling leaves with yellow flowers growing on a vine, used for making a tea; tastes better with lemon, administered at the onset of a cold) then crossed the bridge over the Katabuli creek from which the coldest, clearest spring creek water for drinking was obtained.

By the time I put the sheep to rest, it was time for another visit by the overseer and the saga of the sheep was revived. As I grew older, I promised myself that some way, somehow, someday I would just have to meet these sheep. So on one of my visits to London, I took the train to Scotland even though I could not find a traveling companion for that trip. As soon as we crossed into Scotland, I saw sheep of every color, sheep with black heads and white bodies, brown sheep, black sheep, white sheep. I can't remember if I saw any gray ones, but sheep were everywhere. I was so happy that I was sitting alone because I was smiling from ear to ear. I said out loud "Sheep, I'm pleased to finally meet all of you. I feel as if I have known you all my life." My eyes were riveted to the window, as I tried not to miss a single one.

I don't know if wanting to see the sheep qualifies as a desire of the heart. I was a child who became enthralled by a story being repeated so often, but God did give me that desire. What that tells me is that we serve a God who takes pleasure in granting requests, no matter how insignificant. Jesus is also the good shepherd who cares for sheep and people of all colors. We need to be like Him.

THE QUEEN'S CORONATION

Reference Texts:
Rom. 13:7

Growing up in a British Colony had its advantages e.g. having a day off from school for the sovereigns' birthday or on the birth of a prince or princess, a once in a lifetime coronation or anything to do with the Royalty in Great Britain however far away from there you happened to be. Of course, when the news came over the BBC about King George VI's death, there was just as intense mourning in Guyana as in London. Soon, however, there was excitement in the air as preparations were launched full scale ahead for the coronation of Queen Elizabeth II.

I can still remember the exactness with which Mr. Benn practiced all three area schools to sing the coronation song which had been sent down from England:
"Elizabeth of England as fair as the flowers in spring" etc. (it's been a long time)
Government buildings were being painted, roads repaired, gutters cleaned, bunting in the colors of the Union Jack-red, white, and blue were being hung, the Militia Band practiced every day in the bandstand in the Botanical Gardens and the flurry of activities was enough to make your head spin and take your breath away.

Every morning at school after our morning hymn and prayer, the headmaster lectured us on protocol, respect for the flag and other details such as how neat and clean we should be from head to toe on the day of the coronation. All three schools were supposed to meet at a designated parade ground for the exercises and we were threatened with possible death should we be late for any reason. One morning as we were all standing at attention singing the National Anthem "God Save the Queen", one of my classmates, who was late for school, sauntered in and calmly walked across the floor to her seat. I thought that the headmaster would have had a stroke! He threw his wild cane (an instrument of extreme punishment) at her like a javelin and screamed "You should be shot". The child was so surprised and confused that she

17

started to cry. The rest of us could not show our sympathies. She was to be avoided like the plague for not respecting the flag and the singing of the National Anthem.

June 2nd, 1953 dawned bright and fair at last and folks who were fortunate enough to have radios, had turned the volume way up high to the broadcast from the BBC. Children gathered at the school, the girls wore clean white bodices, maroon pinafore uniforms with pleats sharp enough to do bodily injury to anyone coming too close, ribbons in our hair, white crepe soles (flat canvas shoes) whitened to give the impression of being dipped in milk, and even a brush of face powder which was reserved for some grown ups, but after all, this was coronation day. Even the boys looked almost human in their khaki suits and hair combed for a change. We began marching to the parade grounds with hoards of dressed up grown folks with small flags in their hands. We chatted excitedly wondering what the capitol, Georgetown, could look like, if our little mining town 65 miles away was so transformed. Some people flocked to the churches, church bells were ringing and it was a carnival atmosphere though solemn.

At last the ceremonies began and with speech after speech by members of the clergy, the military, representatives from everywhere, in the heat of the sun compounded by the fact that we had to eat our breakfasts earlier that usual to be on time, many children were soon fainting and dropping like flies. Those of us who were still standing could not voice our opinion, but we were wishing and hoping for an abrupt end to all the ceremonies so that we could move on to the more appealing refreshments. Years later I mused at how oblivious all of this was to the Queen at the time being millions of miles away, it seemed to us, but because we were her subjects, this was the way to show respect and honor even though she was out of sight.

Children, we belong to the Kingdom of God, and although He is out of sight, we still need to reverence Him, remembering that He sees us at all times and in all places. We should "render therefore to all their dues...honor to whom honor is due". He knows what we are going to think about years from now. He does not demand that we stand at attention when in church but He wants us to pay attention and to stop talking and playing while the services are in progress. If you're old enough to read this story, then there is no excuse. God deserves all the honor, praise and glory due to His matchless name. Amen.

NATURE NEEDS NO HELP

Reference Texts:
Psalm 27:14
Rom. 8:18

Occasionally our afternoon classes included a study of nature. We were instructed to bring into class for discussion insects, unusual leaves, germinating seeds or any such forms of nature. The boys were happy to bring in tadpoles, small frogs or worms which would upset some of the girls. On one such occasion, one boy, Dennis, brought in a cocoon he found which had apparently dropped off a leaf or tree trunk. It was decided that he would keep the cocoon at home and report to the class when the butterfly emerged.

Now butterflies are not live carriers, meaning that they do not give birth to little butterflies as a cat gives birth to live kittens. The butterfly lays eggs on the leaf of a tree, after some time the eggs hatch and a caterpillar emerges. The caterpillar has a voracious appetite, eating leaves until it is approximately five times its original size. It then becomes a pupa which is encased in a cocoon of silk which protects it from drying out and from predators. It finally becomes a butterfly. The whole process from egg to butterfly is known as metamorphosis.

For weeks Dennis reported that there had been no activity surrounding the cocoon and even came to the conclusion that the pupa inside might be dead, but the teacher advised him to be patient, knowingly disagreeing with him that the pupa was dead. One Sunday morning Dennis noticed some movement occurring at the tiny end of the cocoon. He watched in excitement as he was able to distinguish the head of the butterfly trying to emerge through what he decided was too small a hole. He took the cocoon outside and called his friend over to see the butterfly before it flew away, but they waited for what seemed like hours and the butterfly had made hardly any progress at all in emerging out of the cocoon. The butterfly seemed to be struggling, taking a very long time and the day was slipping away. The other fellows who did not have such a vested interest in the experiment were becoming restless because they wanted to play some cricket before it was time to do chores.

"I wish this butterfly would hurry up and be born," Saki said, "Did you ever see anything to take such a long time?"

"It can't be much longer," Dennis reassured them, "but if it is not out by the time the horn blows for 12:30pm I think I know a way to help it along."

12:30 came and went and only the complete head of the butterfly had emerged. Had the cocoon been left outside in the atmosphere to be affected by the dew, rain and sun as nature had intended, the cocoon would have been more pliable and able to expand appropriately.

Not wishing to pass up the game Dennis ran inside the house, tiptoed into his mother's bedroom, opened the drawer on the Singer's sewing machine, took out the fine pointed embroidery scissors and rejoined his friends. They all held their breaths as Dennis carefully snipped away at the cocoon enlarging the hole.

Pleased with himself for thinking of the operation his friends extolled his ingenuity. Soon the butterfly had freed herself but what they saw made them retreat in horror, for instead of a beautiful butterfly ready to be airborne, there was a loathsome insect with shriveled up wings and a grotesque swollen, engorged body. This pitiful creature slowly dragged itself around for a few inches and then died. What the boys did not know was that nature intended for the butterfly to force its way slowly out of the cocoon because by so doing the fluids from the body are forced into the wings making the wings large and strong to support the butterfly in its flight.

As children and even as adults, we sometimes encounter situations through which we have to force ourselves. Deliverance comes no other way but going through. Children encounter peer pressure to dress like others, use bad language like others, read books and view television programs which are not wholesome. Adults also encounter trials and situations perhaps on a broader and deeper level, but we all struggle at times. Be careful who you allow to deliver you. The God who created the Universe and all creatures great and small has made a way of escape for everyone who asks Him for help and after our struggles, uncompromised glory shall be revealed in us. Wait patiently on the Lord.

SMART ALEXIS

Reference Texts:
Prov. 4:23
Prov. 26:12
Hos. 8:7

Growing up, respect for everything and everybody was instilled, including respect for clothing. There were three categories of clothing-to be worn as designated-to church, to school, and for play and chores. Because the road was unpaved, our parents decided that we should wear our sturdy school shoes to church for the afternoon services which might involve walking miles to visit sick and "shut-in" members. Maybe I was growing a little tired of all this visiting, so I set about to hatch a plan that would exempt me from going back to services one Sabbath afternoon. Coming home from school that Friday afternoon, we were caught in a downpour of rain, which conveniently aided my dastardly plan, giving me the excuse I needed. I could have taken shelter in the Old Sawmill like we all loved to do when it rained, jumping on the big wheel and shouting in order to hear the echoes, but I ran home through the pouring rain, determined not to avoid any puddles of water as I ran. I then hid my wet shoes way up under the bed.

The next morning dawned bright and fair and I was decked out in my finery wearing my church shoes. Before the close of the service I boasted to a few friends that I would not be back for the afternoon program. Their eyes widened in surprise, with respect for me who, it seemed, was in control of my activities. So they grudgingly bade me goodbye, "We'll see you next week, then."

One of them asked, "So what will you do all afternoon?"

"Oh, anything I like" was the boastful reply as we all went our separate ways for lunch, which was always special for the Sabbath.

When the other children in the home were getting ready to leave, seeing my inactivity, my brother David asked "Vashti, aren't you getting ready?" I knew that he would soon be reporting this to my mother so I took the bold step to her room and said, "Ma, I can't go to church this afternoon because my shoes got wet in the downpour yesterday" I explained.

Without turning around, as cool as a cucumber she said, "Really! And how convenient! And didn't you think to put the shoes to dry near to the oven when you came home?" Turning to face me, whose countenance by this time was like a billboard exposing my deceit, she calmly informed me, "You are going to church this afternoon even if you have to go with your ten commandments (ten toes) on the ground."

I knew that there would be no argument, no discussion, no reversal of the decision, so I started getting dressed. At the last minute I had another bright idea. I put my case to Sister T whose family rented a portion of our house, and good, dear Sister T interceded for me.

"Sis", she pleaded, "give her one more chance, please I'm sure she'll never try anything like this again, let her borrow her church shoes, you know how hard the road is."

I was granted a reprieve but now I had to face the girls at church to whom I had emphatically announced my intentions to be absent that afternoon. On seeing me, they collapsed in laughter and I had no choice but to join in.

They said, "We were wondering if you were crazy or if Sister Hinds had grown soft. You should have known better."

"Well," I explained, "you can't blame me for trying. I really thought that I could get away with this one," revealing the carefully concocted plan involving the wet school shoes. "It was as though my mother saw right through me."

In Prov. 4:23, it encourages us to "keep the heart with all diligence for out of it are the issues of life." When an evil thought or suggestion comes, do not encourage it, nor nourish it. Soon thoughts grow into action. Sow the wind and reap the (good or bad) whirlwind Hos. 8:7. So be careful of every thought which you allow to take root in your mind.

CONVERSION OF THE BULLY

Reference Texts

1 Sam. 11:2

There is an old African proverb which says that it takes a village to raise a child and I'm inclined to agree with it. In our community, the grown ups were revered and respected, we were taught to greet each one we passed on the road, addressing them as Aunt, Uncle, or Cousin, to the point that we did not know who were really our blood relatives. When I began my secondary education in Georgetown, I returned home on the holidays such as Christmas, Easter and the end of the school year, I was obligated to stop by most of the business proprietors who knew my mother to let them know that I was home for the holidays. They inquired as to my grades and encouraged me to adhere to the training they had instilled in me, not to adopt any of the bad behavior they had heard about which took place in Georgetown.

Our next door neighbor was the 6th generation descendant of the Scotsman who settled the area. Everyone called him Uncle or Grandfather and his wife was known as Aunt or Grandmother. Aunt tended a granadilla (Trinidad Barbadine) vine which produced very few fruit (the size of a melon with seeds that look like a passion fruit) maybe once or twice a year, but whenever the granadilla was ripe into each child's mouths was fed a few seeds so that at least we knew what a granadilla tasted like. Likewise when it was time to be purged before school reopened, Aunt administered a dose to every child without ever having to get permission from your mother. If you jumped from too high a

26

tree and hurt yourself, you were diagnosed with having *"NARRA"* and was immediately dispatched to Aunt for a "nointing" (anointing) with crab oil which was produced locally by grating the seed of the crab wood tree (found at the riverside at the Rest House) and placing it in the sun at an angle for the oil to run off and be collected. You tried not to develop NAARA since the odor of the craboil was repugnant, therefore not desirable.

Our church, once or twice a year, held a mini bazaar which was called an Ice Cream Banquet. Items for sale included crocheted doilies, wire and cane baskets, outfits for babies, smocked dressed for girls, knitted socks, small wooden and plaster of Paris wall hangings-all made by the church members. Not to be outdone was the food section offering such delicacies as roti and curry, cassava pone, channa, pineapple tarts, cheese straws, meat patties, plantain chips and mittai (Trinidadian khurma), but the item which drew the crowd was the home made ice cream. The ice cream was made the old-fashioned way-the custard mixture (cooled) was poured into a cylindrical metal container, into which a paddle with attachments was placed with a long piece of metal protruding through the cover to be harnessed to a mechanism with a crank handle. This metal container was then placed in a wooden bucket which was approximately 3" wider in circumference. The space between the metal container and the wooden bucket was packed with ice, to which coarse salt was added to prevent the ice from melting rapidly. At a certain level, there was a small round hole in the wooden bucket so that the water which resulted from the melting ice could safely run off and not get into the metal container with the custard mixture. Children took pleasure in churning the ice cream, (working the crank) because of the hope of reward when the ice cream "came in" (was ready) so children dashed around to the various ladies, imploring to be the one selected to do the churning.

As the bauxite plant expanded families from other areas in Guyana and even some of the West Indian Islands especially St. Lucia, St. Vincent, Barbados, Grenada, Dominica, and from neighboring Suriname moved into the area. It was becoming more difficult to keep up with the parents of some of these children, whose behavior was sometimes atrocious. One such fellow was Robert Nightingale, who was nicknamed "Alexander the Great" or "Robert Night in Jail". His sister, who was a nice girl, tried to reprove and control him as he roamed about freely, slyly being troublesome when the grown ups were not looking. Children went home crying to their parents and he laughed because he knew that by the time the parents came, he would be long gone and, in addition, he was a fast runner. He was especially prone to pick on a little boy named Leon, who avoided him like the plague.

On one such Banquet day, Leon wended his way to the tent where the festivities were being held and applied for and got the position as a churner. He had planned to churn as fast as he could, calculating how many cups of ice cream he could work for in an afternoon. As soon as his first batch was about to "come in" (that's when the crank became stiffer to rotate) who should show up but Alexander the Great!

"Hey Leon" he said gruffly, "either you give me your ice cream or I'll take it from you. Is that understood?" he asked.

"Well alright", Leon replied timidly, not wanting to draw attention to his predicament. The lady came over, opened the ice cream can and although it looked so rich, creamy and inviting, Leon was not excited when she gave him 3 scoops of the ice cream because he knew he was not destined to taste a drop of it. Alexander the Great waited around the corner and grabbed the cup from Leon as soon as the adults were out of sight. He ran a little way off so that he could enjoy his ill gotten gain without interruption.

When he tasted the first mouthful he dropped the cup and spat the ice cream on the ground, "Oh no, what is this? Wait till I catch that no good Leon. What is he trying to do? Poison me?" Apparently, the lid to the metal container was not properly fitted at some time during the process and some of the salt had unwittingly been added to the mixture.

He ran back to the outside of the tent, cursing and accusing Leon of deception and promising to inflict bodily harm on him "tomorrow, tomorrow". What he did not know was that Leon's mother and big brother were on the inside of the tent about 3 feet away. They came out to see what the fuss was about, discovering that Leon was being threatened.

Leon's brother grabbed Robert and his mother looked him in the eye and said, "So you're the Mister Alexander the Great? Well, I don't know your mother but tomorrow tomorrow, I am going to the school and the Police Station and when the Headmaster gets through with caning you, then all of my five big sons will deal with you one at a time and what's left of you, the police can have. Oh! You didn't think that Leon had a family? He didn't drop from a tree you know".

Robert begged, "Sorry Miss Leon, I was only playing with him. Ask him, we're really friends, aren't we Leon? I protect him all the time from the other bad boys. You won't ever find me again saying anything like that again to anybody, not me, Madame! Can your son let go of me now? He's hurting me! Leon, you have a nice mother and brother too," he added as he ran off. From that day onward Robert was the nicest, gentlest boy in the neighborhood and a great friend to Leon!

Even in Bible days there were bullies as we read in 1 Sam. 11:2. Just imagine, Nahash the king of the Ammonites agreeing to make a covenant with the men of Jahesh-Gilead for protection on condition that he first put out the right eyes of all the men in that town (the Ammonites were their relations). King Saul was informed about this plot, the spirit of the Lord came upon him and he delivered the people who were threatened.

Girls and boys, ladies and gentlemen, there are still bullies in all walks and stations of life. Be sure you first let God know about it, involve other agencies, such as the schools, church, and the judicial system because bullying always escalates, so, according to a favorite TV comedian you have to "nip it in the bud."

JOB'S CHICKENS?

Reference Texts
Heb. 2:18
Heb. 4:15

My community was comprised of a number of widows who worked diligently at whatever their hands found to do. One such church sister was Sister Wharton who sold fruits and cassava bread and chocolate sticks. She usually left home very early on mornings to be in position to facilitate her customers who were beginning their jobs at 7 am. One day she intended to run some errands which would have taken up the whole morning and possibly an hour or two after noon. In order that she would not have to do so on returning home tired, hot and hungry, Sister Wharton decided to cook her lunch before leaving home that morning. She covered her meal in the pot and left it on the stove, closing the doors to her kitchen which was separated from the main house.

In those days all animals and livestock roamed free range - cows, sheep, goats, chickens, and ducks. It was interesting to see them coming home on their own before nightfall. Somehow Sister Wharton's chickens made their way into her kitchen, flew up on to the stove, knocked over the pot and ate all the food. To her dismay, when she returned home almost famished, there was not one single grain of rice left for her to eat. Exasperated, he chased the chickens away as she shook her head, sadly saying, "If Job had fowls, he would have sinned." When she repeated the story, even she herself could not help laughing at her outburst at the time. She explained, "The Bible tells you that he had camels, he goats, she goats, oxen and asses, but it didn't mention anything about chickens; If he had only had any chickens like the ones I have, it would have been a different story."

The Bible says that while Jesus was here on earth he suffered everything that we suffer including hunger, tiredness and irritations from man and beast, yet He was without sin. He has also promised us a way of escape that we may be able to bear our temptation - even if it means laughing at our own silly selves. Jesus is our example and He is faithful that promised.

P.S. Sister Wharton always remarked, "What is coming?" I have to wonder the same thing now. I guess she was reading the signs of the times more diligently than other people.

THE LONE RUBBER TREE

References:
2 Tim. 2:19
Psa. 138:8
Isa. 54:17

In a corner of our garden there was an unusual tree; it stood alone, the bark was whitish and it produced an unusual seed encased in a pod which split before it hit the ground. Best of all the tree produced a milky white substance when the bark was scratched. When this substance hardened, it became rubbery and elastic, providing another weapon for childhood pranks. This tree did not produce any edible fruit to justify the space it occupied. There wasn't another tree like it anywhere in the neighborhood, I should know, because I scoured the area on my way to secluded fishing holes and fruit trees. Later on my mother informed me that this was a rubber tree which was protected by the Government. Apparently there must have been rubber plantations in the area; Guyana being on the continent of South America.

The only uses we found for the rubber tree were the rubber which was obtained by chopping the trunk, and using the large seeds, which resembled nutmegs, in our own children's Grocery Store. Our store was well stocked. Living on the banks of a river, sand was everywhere, so we used it to represent sugar, salt, rice and flour. We stocked baby coconuts, the red sheath (navel) from the banana plant served as the meat and so on and so on (use your imagination). Quite insidiously, the tree began leaning towards our house until it became quite noticeable. I guess we had drained most of the rubber out of it, but we were not going to miss the tree when

it was cut down which we, the children, thought we could do without much effort. I can't tell you how my mother knew all these things, but she went to the Commissary Office and reported what was happening with the tree and after visits by the Ranger and subsequent paper work, someone was assigned to cut down the tree and remove the trunk.

Several years later remembering this tree, it brought to mind how alone a person could feel at times, thinking that no one else knows where you are or what you are going through, but just how this tree was protected by the Government, and that it could not even be cut down without permission to avoid falling on a house, causing damage, it is comforting to know that God knows where you are and that no weapon formed against you shall prosper. My most favorite Bible verse is found in Psalm 138:8 "The Lord will perfect that which concernth Me." When I discovered this verse, I had the feeling of discovering diamonds or the most precious metal on earth. I felt so highly favored of the Lord, like I was the only one on earth. The Bible also says that the Lord knows them that are His. We need to focus on making sure that we know that we belong to Him.

THE DISAPPEARING PEANUT BRITTLES

Reference Texts:
Exod. 20:
Acts 5:1-11

I have always been a lover of any kind of nut or anything made from nuts that it was no surprise that I found myself in deep trouble with my mother when I was probably around 8 years old. At school we broke for lunch at 11:30am after saying and singing "Grace before meals." We walked home for lunch, ate and hurried back to school before the bell rang; hurrying back as soon as we could in order to play in the yard, or on the swings. The boys played their own version of cricket with bats made out of coconut branch heads and the fruit of the Etae palm serving as the ball. Children, usually the girls, who were rich enough to have a cent (1 c) or a penny (2 c) gained lots of friends because, sitting with trays outside the school compound, were women selling dainties such as fudge, green mangoes with salt and pepper, sugar cakes and channa (salted chick peas), custard blocks, butterscotch and stretcher. If your friend had any money at least you were promised a "bite" of whatever your friend bought.

My mother was an absolute business woman so she seized the opportunity to enter the competition by supplying an item which no one else sold. We're talking about Peanut Brittle. She blanched the nuts in their red sheaths; we peeled off the skin and then she made the brittle, cutting it up into squares which would sell for one cent or one penny. There was a large, square, red metal container with a bouquet of roses etched on the metal, which had previously held cookies. In those days most of our goods came from England and New Zealand, even our cheese.

My mother would put the whole batch of brittles into this large container, dispensing a small amount into a smaller container for me to take to school for sale. Loving nuts as I did, it was a grave temptation to return the unsold portion to the large container every day, so I ate a few pieces and put back just the minimum so that at least I could say that I put the unsold portion back.

I think my mother began to suspect what was going on since hardly any money was coming in, but she let me play the game waiting to see how long it would take for me to implicate myself. One fine day she gave me the small container with the brittles, and after only selling a few I ate all the rest. When my mother asked me what I did with the rest, I told her, like I always did, that I had returned them to the large container, whereupon she opened the container and I stared into space. How was I to know that she had given me the last of the batch?

Well, I had to listen to a long lecture on Ananias and Sapphira, I was called an "eye servant" Eph. 6:6 I was reminded in no uncertain terms "Be sure your sins will find you out." My mother did not mind my eating of the brittle, in fact, she let me have some every day, but she was disappointed that I did not speak the truth. I was so embarrassed that I almost refused my supper. I learned a good lesson that day about the importance and simplicity of speaking the truth. Needless to say, that was the end of that venture. I also had to learn the following verse:

> Speak the truth and speak it ever
> Cost it what it will,
> He who hides the wrong he does
> Does the wrong thing still.

Remember children, honesty is the best policy.

THE TRUANT OFFICER

References:
Matt. 24:42, 44-46

One fine day my brother, David, and my cousin, Joseph Daniels, nicknamed "Danny Kaye" decided to skip school. They probably had not completed their homework assignments which consisted of learning a host of parables which did not appear to make sense, or one of the poems located at the back of the Nelson's West Indian Reader by J.O. Cutteridge. When we left home for school, they lagged behind, not keeping in step with the group; they even fell back behind the children who came from the opposite bank of the river by corial or ballahoo (paddle-operated canoes). When the coast was clear, they dashed off towards the path leading to Bucktown. The rest of us had no idea that they were absent since we were being taught in different classrooms.

They played to their hearts' content (later reported) trying to catch birds, chasing lizards, playing with tadpoles in the small estuaries of the main creek, picking and eating cashews, cocorite and edible-looking berries. In short, they were having a high, old time. Time flew quickly as it usually does when you're having fun, and soon they were startled by the horn which announced the 11 o'clock hour. They reckoned that it was time to leave Bucktown and get close to the road to blend in with the children going home for lunch at 11:30. They did not plan to miss any meals that day, only classes.

They came out of the forest, furtively glancing up and down the road which was void of grown ups. They then took up their positions crouching behind the "Carrion Crow" brushes waiting for the children to get closer (it would have raised questions had they arrived home for lunch before the rest of the children). As they heard the squeals of delight as the children approached, they very cautiously arose out of their hideaway and you'll never guess who was walking past them at that very moment! Yes, my mother! Of all the days of the week, they chose to do this on a Wednesday, totally forgetting that all the businesses is the area closed after the morning trading hours on Wednesdays.

You can quite imagine their confusion as they stuttered to explain their positions. The gig was up! No explanations were necessary. My mother commanded them to "March!" and the pair sheepishly walked ahead of her to the jeers of the school children who had now caught up with them. What ensued was a counselling session embellished with manual emphasis (ask your parents for explanations). Suffice it to say, they ate their lunches standing up. They were also sent back to school with a note to the Headmaster which gained them a second helping (definitely not of lunch).

"Watch therefore...for in such an hour as ye think not the Son of man cometh...Blessed is that servant, whom when his Lord cometh shall find so doing" the Bible cautions. As long as we're doing the right thing, we do not have to fear discovery by anyone. We have the confidence that God is well pleased with our lives and we can hold our heads up high encouraging others to be ready for HIs soon coming.

WHO'RE YOU GOING TO CALL?

Reference Texts:
Acts 4:12
Psalm 50:15
Ex. 20:3-6
Psalm 124:8

By this time, boys and girls, you are aware that travel in Guyana in the days of my childhood was mostly by boats of all sizes. There was one rather interesting mode of travel - a vessel which looked almost like a sail boat but operated by an engine - called a schooner. They were mostly used for transporting goods from Georgetown to the Essequibo county by way of the Essequibo River which was 19 miles wide at its mouth (believe it). To get to the mouth of the Essequibo River from Georgetown which was at the mouth of the Demerara River, the schooners had to sail along the west coast of Demerara thereby encountering a portion of the Atlantic Ocean.

Travel by schooner was not for the faint of stomach or heart. Passengers were herded below deck; only the brave sailors stayed on deck to "batten down the hatches" and do what else sailors do. The schooner always left Georgetown at 5am, so as children, we were sometimes awakened at 1am in order to be on time for departure. We would have loved to have a good breakfast but our parents wisely allotted us just a morsel to keep us going. We had a good idea as to how rough the journey would be, but we were overjoyed at going to visit relatives, so we acted as though the expected roughness of the voyage was of no consequence at all.

Our parents settled us down by making us little beds to sleep on should we desire, and soon after the engine started we could hear the sailors shouting and running on deck as they cast off from the stelling (pier). We were on our way and everything was going smoothly, only an occasional gentle rocking motion of the schooner reminded us that we were approaching the open sea. Soon the rocking became more noticeable and the sound of the waves as it clashed against the bow of the schooner was audible. This motion increased in intensity and all passengers began to look at each other with concern, children with fear, some even crying and/or emptying the contents of their stomachs for which their parents were prepared.

Passengers were of all races and religions. There were passengers of African descent, East Indians, American Indians, some Chinese and Portuguese. Some of them made the sign of the cross, some prayed aloud, but there was this one woman of East Indian descent who sat alone dressed in traditional ornate sari, thick gold bangles (bracelets) around her ankles, bracelets on her arms, rings in her ears and nose. She tried to appear calm, but when the motion of the schooner increased she would pray aloud to her gods as she rocked from side to side. She alternated between calling on Rama and Krishna every time a huge wave hit the schooner.

The schooner was now being tossed about violently adding to the despair of the darkness outside. The lady of whom I spoke previously had intensified her prayer "Oh Rama," she implored, "Oh Krishna," she interceded each time a big wave hit.

Suddenly a tremendous, gigantic wave hit. All lights went out as the engine sputtered into silence amid the frantic shouts of the sailors. Passengers screamed and prayed, but this time the lady screamed in terror "O Lord, O God, O Jesus Christ!" Even amid the chaos it was amusing because we knew that she was not taking God's name in vain. She obviously had heard about the true and living God before but had chosen to cling to her traditional gods. In this life and death situation, she came face to face with the fact that Rama and Krishna could do nothing, so she called on the true and living God.

The Bible says that if we call on the name of the Lord we would be saved and there is "No other name under heaven, given among men whereby we must be saved." We are also commanded to have no other gods before God Almighty. Let us not wait until we find ourselves in dire straights before believing and calling on the name of the Lord. He invites us to call upon Him in the time of trouble and He promises to deliver us.

A CASE OF RACE

Reference Texts:
Prov. 17:17 & 18:24
Luke 7:34
James 2:23

"What you looking' at?" Peter scowled at James, the lone Native American Indian (called Amerindians in Guyana) in his class. James bowed his head and did not reply. Since the school term began James always seemed to irritate Peter even when he wasn't doing or saying anything.

"Why are you always picking on James, what has he done to you?" asked Oscar.

"Nothing" Peter confessed, "I just don't like him. He is too quiet. I don't trust quiet people."

"That's no reason to dislike him. His people don't usually say much, but they know a lot of things. Everybody is good for something. Leave him alone." Oscar advised.

"All that may be true, but I still don't like him," was Peter's comment.

"Forget about James, I'll see you tomorrow for the cricket match.", was Oscar's reply.

All the children started for home, James walking alone behind the group of children, trying to avoid Peter at all cost. At the Old Sawmill, James turned off the path on the left going towards his home in a settlement called Bucktown. Peter's little brother, a first grader, affectionately called Boogie by everybody turned around and saw James taking the path and innocently asked "Where is he going?"

"He's going to Bucktown. That's where "they" live. I hear 'they" have no furniture; "they" lie in hammocks all day. Don't you see? He doesn't wear shoes, so he must have chiggers. Don't play with his little sister either" Peter instructed.

"Why?" asked Boogie.

"Because you may catch something. I think they have lice too. Besides, mind your business and come along home."

In those days, there were 6 races of people living in Guyana. The Amerindians are the indigenous people. They were mostly Carib and some Arawak. The Dutch made contracts with the Indians in 1580, settling Essequibo in 1621 and Berbice in 1651 (two of the three counties). The British attempted to drive out the Dutch in 1665 and the French also failed in their attempt in 1708. In 1678 shipments of African slaves arrived in British Guiana as it was then known. In 1814 the territory was ceded to Britain by the Treaty of Utrecht. Slavery was abolished in 1838. The Portuguese arrived in 1841, ten years afterwards, in 1851, the East Indians arrived as indentured laborers, having the option to return to India but, most of them stayed. In 1853, the Chinese arrived and in 1966, after 152 years of British rule Guyana received its Independence.

As children we were not very interested in all the history and for the most part we were color blind, but occasionally the devil would stir something up as was the case with Peter against James.

The next day Peter joined his friends for a lively game of cricket on a strip of ground behind the houses. He heard his mother calling, "Peter, come and take Boogie outside with you. I'm trying to sew some curtains and he is getting in the way. Keep an eye on him, you hear?"

"Yes Ma," Peter shouted his reply, not really relishing the idea of having to watch Boogie when the game was so interesting.

When the 5:45pm horn sounded, his mother, Miss Irene, called them in, "It's time to come in now boys, wash your face and hands and come in for your supper."

Peter looked around for Boogie and rubbed his eyes in disbelief when he did not see him sitting under the tree where he had definitely told him to stay. Peter frantically ran around to the neighbors asking if Boogie had been to their houses but, everyone he asked said "No" and he felt a lump in his throat as fear seized him. He ran to the riverside where some girls were playing on the beach. He was breathless as he asked Gloria "Was Boogie here with you all?"

"Of course not!" Gloria replied, "this was for girls only. You boys play cricket by yourselves, don't you?"

"I don't have time to argue, Gloria, I can't find Boogie" and with that said, he ran off because he heard his mother calling and threatening this time.

"Don't make me come out there for you, Peter, bring Boogie inside. He must be more than hungry now. If your father comes home and you are not in this house, I don't have to tell you what you can expect."

Peter knew now that he had to face his mother with the awful truth. He could not bear the thought of his father being added to the mix. He burst into the yard; his mother was standing on the veranda, he blurted out "Ma, I can't find Boogie."

"Oh Lord", she screamed and fell to the floor, "Boogie is lost, we can't find Boogie," she wailed.

The neighbors rushed over trying to comfort her and at the same time asking for details.

"What happened?" they asked Irene.

"I don't know. Ask Peter" she was now rolling on the veranda, pulling at her hair and clothes. "I hope that the Bush Dai Dai, Kanaima or Massacuraman (folklore spirits of the forest and the river) didn't take my child. A child disappeared just like that the other day in Dalgin and up to now nobody knows what happened."

"Don't talk like that, Irene. Peter, did you check down by the river?" asked Miss Jones.

Irene, sitting on the steps and holding her abdomen wailed, "Lord what am I going to tell Ovid when he comes home in a few minutes?" where upon a child shouted, "I think I see him coming now."

Ovid, apprehensive at the crowd gathered on the road in front of the house, sprang off his bicycle, dropped it and ran into the yard. Before he could ask a question one of the neighbors volunteered the information "Boogie is lost."

"What? When? Where? How? Who last saw him? Anybody looking for him?" he exploded. He was brought up to date on the information available. He instructed "Send someone to the Ranger's House. I will ride back to the Police Station. Maybe they would organize some Scouts to help us. Are you all sure that he didn't go to the river?" They again assured him and he was off to the Police Station at break neck speed.

By this time it was dark and the only light available to him came from the headlight of his bicycle. When he reached the Katabuli Bridge, his headlight outlined an older Amerindian boy holding Boogie's hand walking towards him.

"Boogie! Boogie!" he screamed in delight, almost in tears as he sprang off his bicycle.

"Daddy, Daddy" Boogie screamed back as they raced towards each other and were locked in an embrace which lasted several minutes.

"Are you alright, Boogie?" kissing him all over. Ovid now turned his attention to the boy who was turning to leave. "Wait, son" he said, "thanks for bringing Boogie home. Where did you meet him?"

"He came to Bucktown all by himself, so I thought I would bring him home myself because I know him and I didn't want him to be lost."

"I really appreciate this. My whole family and neighborhood was pretty much torn up over this. As a matter of fact I was on my way to the Police station to report him missing."

"It was nothing. He's a nice kid."

"Son, what's your name?"

"James, Sir. Peter is my best friend at school."

"Well, thank you, James and please say thanks to your parents for allowing you to bring him home. Please accept this small token of our appreciation" Ovid said, offering him some money.
"Oh no! like I said, Peter is my very best friend. Good night to you sir. See you at school Boogie." he said, waving goodbye.

"Can I walk at least part of the way back with you?" Ovid asked.

"That won't be necessary. I am at home out here at all times of the day and night. You'd better take Boogie home. They might still be looking for him."

"I guess you're right. Take care now." With that being said, Ovid placed Boogie on the handlebar of the bicycle and raced back to the house excitedly ringing his bicycle bell and shouting, "I found Boogie, I found Boogie." Cheers went up as Boogie bounded towards his mother, who went into a higher octave of sobs. No one was happier to see Boogie more than Peter, who was jumping up and down, pressing his father for details of his recovery.

Ovid began, "You know, Peter, that's the kind of friend I like to see you keeping company with. Boogie walked all the way to Bucktown by himself. Luckily your best friend James saw him and was bringing him home. I met them at the bridge. I offered him some money, but he wouldn't hear of it, he insisted that being your best friend was good enough for him. Peter, how come you never invited James to come home with you to even play a game? That's how friends should live. What a nice boy!"

Peter was thankful that it was dark, so that the remorse could not be seen on his face. He had treated James so shamefully for no reason yesterday and today James had saved the life of his brother and most certainly his own.

The Bible clearly states that God made all nations of men of one blood to dwell upon the face of the earth and has determined the bounds of their habitation. In a vision the Apostle Peter was advised against calling anything or anyone common or unclean, Jesus shed His precious blood for everyone therefore, no person is better than the other. We are all in need of a Savior regardless of race, color, religion, gender or nationality.

Remember everyone is good for something!
Monday morning…
"Ma, please make a few extra bakes this morning. I really want to take a few for my best friend James" Peter asked, and Boogie and Ovid agreed wholeheartedly.

AUNTIE'S TITHE/MITE

Reference Texts
Matt. 3:10,11

I was brought up on the West Bank of the Demerara River across from the mining town known in those days as Mackenzie (now called Linden after President Linden Forbes Burnham, who was Prime Minister when Guyana achieved independence in 1966). In the later 1700's the area consisted of plantations producing suger cane, coffee, cocoa and lumber, but in 1914 a Scotsman visited the area pretending to be interested in planting oranges, so he bought almost 4,000 acres of land from descendants of R.F. Allicock and the other Scottish land owners, also taking soil samples which he claimed he needed to verify the suitability of the land for the oranges.

What the families were unaware of was that previous soil samples had detected traces of an important ore called Bauxite and now Mr. Mackenzie (George Bain), who was indeed a geologist, was sent by foreign investors to further explore and secure the land. The deception was discovered too late: the area became known as Mackenzie (obviously named in his honor). Soon large ships were plying the waters up to Mackenzie, first to transport the heavy equipment including cranes for excavation and removal of the overburden (top soil and sand) laying tracks for locomotives and cars, building and installing kilns and all related machinery to process the ore, then later to transport the ore to Canada and other parts of the world. This could not have happened at a

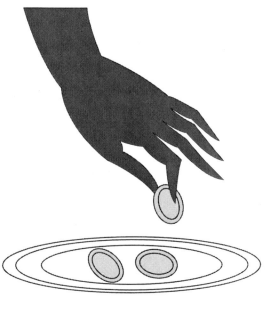

46

better time for Mackenzie because bauxite was used in the production of aluminum needed for airplanes and ships which were in great demand in World War I, also used for making household wares.

Most of the men in the area worked at the bauxite plant. It was a 24/7 operation, very noisy, to say the least. There was a loud, throaty horn (later replaced by a siren) which could be heard for miles sounding to awaken the workmen at 5:30am, then at 6:50am to let them know that they had 10 minutes in which to be ferried across with bicycles, helmets, goggles. It was always a flurry of excitement at the boat landing early in the morning. The horn sounded again at 11am for lunch, then 12:20pm to remind them to be back to work for 12:30pm, then again at 4:30pm when the day shift ended and again at 5:45pm, I guess to remind children that it was time to be inside the house. In addition to the steady day shift Monday to Friday 7:00am-4:30pm, there were 3 shifts 7:00am-3:00pm, 3:00pm-11:00pm, and 11:00pm-7:00am so that the operation continued uninterrupted.

At such a plant there was no pantry or microwave (not yet invented) so the men who started working at 7am had their lunches sent by their wives in time for the 11:00am lunch break. These lunch carriers consisted of 2 or 3 compartments of metal or enamel bowls held together by a two pronged metal frame with a handle. These were picked up at the homes and taken to the gate outside the plant by women who did this for a living.

My Aunt Orpah was one of these women. She was a widow and her three children had all predeceased her. She therefore had to make a living somehow, as she was also taking care of some of her grandchildren. To supplement her income from transporting the lunches, she sold bananas, ground cocoa beans and rolled them into chocolate sticks (for making hot cocoa) made and sold cassava bread which is made with Yucca flour farina. She liked to make the smaller sweet version with sweetened, stewed coconut in the middle. She needed to be resourceful since the plant only paid wages once monthly so that there were at least 3 out of 4 weeks that she had no money except what she made from sales.

She was a faithful tither despite her situation. I remember that one Sabbath she paid a tithe of 3c and believe me, it meant that she had only worked for 30c that week. She was not one to complain to people about her situation; you would never know if she had nothing to eat.

She was one of the first ones at church, singing lustily in her Barbadian accent. When I received my first paycheck of $95.00 after one full month of hospital work, my mother divided my whole check among my aunts and all the elderly at the church and in the community. On immigrating to the USA, I occasionally sent small monetary gifts and kept in touch however I could, visiting her on my visits to Guyana.

While living in North Carolina, one day I received a call from her pastor telling me that she was in need of help due to the Nationalization of the bauxite plant after Independence, ensuing retrenchment of workers and the general deterioration of the area. My brother and I decided to support her monthly as she was being cared for by her granddaughter who could not work and care for her at the same time. She had also lost her sight. She instructed someone to write to thank us. When I visited her in 1994, I received her blessings and made arrangement for the inevitable. Immediately my mind went back to the time that she gave the tithe/mite of 3c, with the best attitude. The Psalmist David remarked that he had never seen the righteous forsaken or the Lord's seed begging bread. It was marvelous to see that although she was widowed, and predeceased by all her children, the Lord provided for her even though it was from a country far away. She lived to a ripe old age of 95. God always honors His word. He says that heaven and earth will pass away before one "jot or tittle" of His word falls to the ground, and He always means what He says.

LET NOT THE SUN GO DOWN

Reference Texts:
Matt. 6:9-15
Eph. 4:26

Two of my female cousins being raised by my mother in the early 1960's enjoyed a congenial relationship for the most part. They enjoyed pleasing Aunt Winnie, sometimes competing for her attention and approval. At Christmas time, baking the fruit cake was a big production as one of them would cream the butter and sugar and the other would wisk the eggs (all by hand, of course). My mother often found herself in the middle of having to divide up the scant amount of cake batter waiting to be "licked" out of the mixing bowl. She therefore devised a plan to eliminate the frustration of serving them the cake after it was baked. Each one was given an individual cake to be eaten at that person's discretion; should you be impressed to eat the whole cake in one day, the pleasure was yours, or if you wanted to trade or make a deal with a part of your cake it was up to you. My mother controlled the cake to be offered to company visiting; no one knew where she kept it.

Daphne's cake had been long gone and she looked on longingly as Ezme ate hers in slivers every day for dessert. One day, when Ezme was down to her last slice, the two cousins were having lunch together but Daphne was busily devising a plan to at least have some of it. It looked so moist and succulent that her salivary glands were working overtime. Suddenly she said, "Look, Ezme" pointing to the living room, "A bird just flew in the window," and as Ezme turned to look, Daphne snatched the cake and gobbled it down. Ezme flew into a rage when she discovered that she had been duped and, because fighting was forbidden she stormed out of the house vowing never to forgive Daphne.

Ezme sought refuge at quite a good distance away from the house. On her way there she passed a neighbor, Miss Edna, who looked at her until she was out of sight. To add insult to injury, the fish were not "biting" (the bait)so she returned home, only to be confronted by Miss Edna sitting in her Aunt's rocking chair, reporting that she had seen her going to an area that was dangerous for a girl to go alone. This was the last straw; she already had put Daphne on her Unforgiveness List, now Miss Edna would have to be added on, but she could not openly show her hatred since Miss Edna was a grown up. Ezme concluded that nothing had worked out right for her at all that day.

Ezme continued nursing the unforgiveness in her heart, though she was found to act friendly when Aunt Winnie was around. Every night at evening worship when "The Lord's Prayer" was repeated, she was silent when the prayer reached the part "And forgive us our trespasses as we forgive those who trespass against us." The memory verse for that week also tugged at her heart strings, Eph. 4:56 "Be ye angry, and sin not, let not the sun go down on your wrath." She rationalized that the verse did not apply to her; she had good reason to be angry.

Visitors from Trinidad were expected and the day finally came for the trip to the airport to meet Tante Liley and Mrs. Thomas. Daphne and Ezme sat in the back seat of the car, each looking out windows on opposite sides. It was exciting to be going to the airport and seeing the airplanes and arriving passengers; there would also be some snacks which were not available in their neck of the woods.

Soon the flight's arrival was announced, the airplane zoomed on to the runway, circled at the end of the field and stopped on the tarmac in front of the tower. On exiting the visitors were introduced and welcomed, loaded into the waiting car which drove out of the terminal, gaining speed after merging with the traffic on the main road. Everyone was chatting gaily. Ezme almost forgot her anger while trying to decipher the new accent of the visitors, when all of a sudden, there was the shrill screeching of brakes as the car was forced off the road by a discourteous driver. The car somersaulted down the bank three times, spun around, with the trunk and back seat of the car actually submerged in the river. The front wheel of the car, being caught in a tree stump, was the only thing preventing the total submersion of the car.

Ezme found herself tightly locked in Daphne's protective grip, both girls screaming at the top of their voices (along with the adults) for help.

Soon there were excited shouts from people who had witnessed the accident and brought the needed assistance. Men were seen running towards the car shouting "Hold on, hold on. Don't move. We'll get you out." Assessing the situation, it was decided that it would be better to get the occupants out of the car first before trying to pull the car back on land. Miraculously there were no physical injuries, but the girls sat on the bank visibly shaken, but thankful for God's protection which had been implored before leaving the airport.

It was now time for Ezme to confess that she had been harboring unforgiveness in her heart since the incident with the cake. Daphne asked for forgiveness for her involvement and they both thanked God that they were given a chance to ask and receive forgiveness. They both realized that the accident could have been fatal and they vowed that from that day onward they would not allow the sun to do down on their wrath with anyone.

FOR LACK OF VISION

Reference Texts:
Psalm 35:27
Prov. 29:18

This story is a testimony to the goodness of God, His faithfulness to provide and the bond which existed between the McIntosh sisters. My Aunt Beulah became ill, rendering her unable to care for herself or her children. My mother, being the oldest sister having promised Mama to keep the family together, took the two preteens to live with us and sent the toddler to live with the eldest child who was already being cared for by one of our great aunts. It was a case of "the more, the merrier" at our house, so it did not matter how many cousins came together, to us it signaled more fun. My mother was known to bring old ladies who did not have relatives to our home to be cared for until she could locate some other willing caregiver. The most famous of these was Tanta who promptly reported any and every act of misbehavior the moment my mother came home.

Danny Kaye (as he was nicknamed) enjoyed elementary school, but when it became time to attend high school he proudly announced to my mother that he was not going to attend. She was no licensed psychologist but she realized that due to a lack of a positive male role model in his life, he was experiencing problems with his self esteem. She discussed the situation with the headmaster who affirmed that he was rather intelligent and was appalled at the possibility that he might torpedo his future. My mother secured a part time job for him making deliveries for the local baker. He was in his element, riding the bicycle with the large carrier basket in front that he just knew that he had realized his life's ambition.

The Headmaster suggested that Danny Kaye should come to his home for school lessons in the evenings. He was introduced to such subjects as Algebra, Geometry, advanced English courses and to coin a phrase he took to those subjects like "duck to water."

My mother's brain was actively making plans to harness his intelligence and creativity. The sisters discussed his enrolment in Caribbean Union

College in Trinidad. Pledges of support were obtained from the financially able. My Aunt Beryl who was the district midwife at Dora at the time arranged to send her share of money out to my mother when the steamer stopped on its way to the town. The money was secured in an envelope and given to my cousin Neil who was supposed to join the canoe going out to the steamer in mid

Joseph and wife Bibi playing a game he designed

river. Mail was usually exchanged and ground provisions and coal were loaded on to the steamer for delivery in Georgetown. Neil played by the riverside until the steamer was in sight and the horn sounded, but when he met my mother she motioned to my aunt on the shore that Neil did not have the money with him. When he came ashore my aunt cut a switch and chased him off to find the envelope with the money which was found floating in the river close by the other children and grown ups.

Danny Kaye soon boarded an airplane to Trinidad to attend a boarding school offering secondary and tertiary levels of education. Within two years he completed his secondary education. He then entered college, graduating in 1966 with an Associate of Arts Degree.

He returned to Guyana for a while and taught in schools in Georgetown and Parima in the interior of Guyana. He later immigrated to the USA where he completed his Bachelor's and Master's degrees in science, later completing nursing degrees with CCRN certification. He was also featured in a local West Coast newspaper and interviewed on CBS channel 6 for designing a card game called "Touch Four King."

The Lord takes pleasure in the prosperity of his servants, but where there is no vision, the people perish. Sometimes a suggestion or encouragement is all that is needed to point someone in the right direction. Patience is also needed when things seem to be moving slowly. May we be aware of individuals who would greatly benefit from an encouraging word and prayer.

MANWICH FROM HEAVEN

Reference Texts
Exod. 16:14-18
Phil. 4:19

Boys and girls, I know that you have heard the story of how God fed the children of Israel with manna during their wilderness wanderings and also how He fed Elijah by the ravens and the widow of Zerephat, well I'm here to inform you that he is still doing the same thing today.

In 1955, I qualified for a West Demerara scholarship on taking my CXC (called the Common Entrance in those days). This scholarship offered more than the usual because it provided books and uniforms; in addition to the high school fees for the year. In Guyana in those days, high school education was the responsibility of the parents. Many children  were unable to attend because, added to the schools fees, was the cost of transportation, meals, sometimes boarding, which became a heavy burden especially if two or more children were in high school at the same time.

The scholarship dictated that I should attend a Roman Catholic Convent High School. There was such an outcry from my local congregation being a Seventh Day Adventist church, some members even suggested that my mother should refuse the scholarship. My mother flatly refused, thanked them for their concerns, soliciting their prayers and affirmed that she knew me to be well grounded enough to attend any parochial school. I left home with strong warnings against intercession of Saints, bowing to statues and the infallibility of the Pope. I was not a least bit concerned about all these things. I was a child about to embark on a wonderful new experience, although somewhere in the back of my mind I knew that these two religions were diametrically opposed to each other.

I soon settled into the school routine, amazed at the difference in religious teachings. The sophistication was also far removed from my elementary school mates at the Church of Scotland school I had just left behind. Listening to the stories about the saints was new to me, also the practice sessions for the May Crowning, but I did come to learn to love St. Joseph really well since he was the Patron Saint of our school, giving us a day off on his feast day. I adopted an attitude of "live and let live." Religion was not being forced on me, I participated in what I conscientiously could but, I was still aware of the differences. At lunch break the tennis tables were dominated by certain girls who later became the country's tennis champions. My little group of friends sat under the stairs discussing girl things or the Song Corner. Oh yes! The words to the top tunes were printed in the Sunday papers, cut out and brought to school by girls whose parents subscribed to the newspaper. We were always up on the latest songs.

Before the advent of "High Five," we greeted each other with "Cuz, Cuz, how you does?" and the idiotic reply would be "Just the same as I used to was!" at which we would roll with laughter.

We did a lot of pranks such as rearranging our desks or wall hangings on days that we did not want to hear about "The Prisoner of Chillon" or "Peter Grimes", because we knew that when Sister Patricia came into the room she would stop midway through the prayer and lecture us up to within five minutes of the end of the period. One day a lay teacher asked, "What's a ferret?" My mother always encouraged me to read, so I was the only one who knew that the ferret was a small domesticated animal. Needless to say, my nickname became "Ferret" from that day onward. Suffice it to say that Ferret and her friends were having a high old time as Convent High School girls.

My allowance was $1.00 per week which was a lot of money in those days. I still had change left over after buying lunch for 8c a day - 5c for a big chunk of cheese or a big glob of peanut butter on a tennis roll and 3c for a lemonade. Tragedy struck one day and I had no money for lunch. I needed to repair a puncture in a tire of my bicycle which took all the money I had. The prospect of not having any lunch, sitting through the afternoon session, riding my bicycle to the train station, riding the train for another 45 minutes, then walking home from the train, filled me with dismay but I was determined to endure my little cross all by myself.

When class dismissed for lunch that day I remained at my desk. While putting away her materials, my homeroom nun asked, "Vashti, aren't you going to lunch?"

"In a minute, Sister Edith, I want to catch up on some things first."

"Very well then," she said, disappearing down the hall going towards the cloister for her lunch. In about 10 minutes she came back and expressed her surprise at seeing me still there. "Vashti, are you still here?"

"Yes, Sister Edith, I'll be finished soon," I replied, the hunger pangs starting to kick mercilessly.

She again left and the next time the door opened Sister Edith was bringing me the largest, juiciest sandwich I had ever seen up to that time in my life. I thanked her, my children thanked her and God although they did not know it at the time. Thus at the ripe old age of 12. I came to the conclusion that it is not what or who you say you are, but it is what you do that counts. Religions separate people but Jesus invites us to be a part of His kingdom. "And my God shall supply all my needs according to His riches in glory by Jesus Christ."

BE CAREFUL LITTLE LIPS

Reference Texts
John 15:12
James 3:5

As a teenager attending High School, on Sundays I sometimes visited friends in the neighboring villages. This particular Sunday I decided to visit my friend Grace in Beterverwagting (BV) who was more like a sister to me since neither of us was blessed with having natural sisters. Looking for something exciting to do, we decided on having my hair pressed (straightened with a hot comb). I needed to have permission from my mother anyway but I told her that it was all right. Her mother, Aunt May brought us the combs and sat looking at us, taking in the Sunday afternoon atmosphere. After shampooing and drying the hair, it was parted into four sections, shoulders draped with a towel and the adventure began. When one half of my hair was pressed, I believe it was a question about "holding the ears" when I gave her quite a rude answer . She immediately announced that she was finished with my hair, refusing to press the other half.

Well, you could quite imagine my predicament but I was not about to beg. I acted as if it didn't matter, while she roared with laughter, guessing my confusion. In addition to not having permission, how could I present myself to my mother with my hair half done? (the old people would have called me a half-picked duck) I picked up a newspaper, biding my time, deciding what to do. When I saw that she had no intention of relenting I gathered my stuff to go home. When I went to the living room to say "goodbye" to Aunt May, who was playing the organ out there, she spun around in surprise asking "What happened to your hair?"

I recounted details of the falling out where upon she said "Pay her no mind, girl, I'll finish your hair for you." When Aunt May's back was turned, I stuck my tongue out at Grace in triumph.

It has been at least fifty years since that day; we are still sisters. The Bible teaches us to love one another and to be aware of what a big fire the small tongue can kindle. Let us endeavor to control our tongues and maintain our friendships. We used to sing a little song. The words went like this:

Be careful little lips what you say
Be careful little lips what you say
For your Father up above
Is looking down with love
So be careful little lips what you say

There were other verses:
Be careful little eyes what you see...
Be careful little ears what you hear...
Be careful little feet where you go...

Just be careful!

"A Camping We Did Go"

In the good old days, the believers came together for a weekend every year which came to be known as Federation. This was in the days of the pioneers of the establishment of the Seventh - day Adventist church in British Guiana. I was very young at the time but names such as Pastor McEchrane, Pastor Greaves, Pastor Carrington, Pastor "Nattie" Payne, were often spoken of with respect and admiration.

Later on more emphasis was placed on the younger people with the advent of Youth's Congress and other related group meetings. Week-long camps were then held at Atkinson Air Field (now Cheddi Jagan Airport) and weekend retreats at Bootooba (approximately 20 miles up river from McKenzie/Wismar). Soon Camp Goshen (near Bartica in the Essequibo) was purchased and permanent cabins and a meeting house, a kitchen and other facilities were constructed. By that time, even the pre-teens were becoming adventurous and the parents were becoming more supportive of the fine leadership exhibited by such Pastors as Earl Parchment, Milton Nebblett, Adrian Westney and Lionel Arthur, that it was decided to have junior and senior camps a week apart. For that first year, due to unforeseen circumstances the juniors and seniors had to be combined, making it a total enrollment of 105 campers.

Waiting for the rafts at Amatuk Falls August 1959

The excitement was too much to contain as the time approached. Campers traveled from Berbice and Demerara the day before in order to be aboard the boat for Bartica leaving at 5am. Some were dressed in uniforms denoting the rank of Friends, Companions, Guides or Master Guides (later changed to Pathfinders). Although the traveling was slightly turbulent along the West Coast of the Demerara before entering into Essequibo River, when the boat stopped at Parika, we were happy to see the campers joining us from the islands of Leguan and Wakenaam, Anna Catherina and other villages on the coast. It was very intriguing to observe the hustle and bustle on the Stelling as porters loaded and unloaded merchandise, and vendors plied their wares.

Our next stop was at Fort Island where remains of the Dutch Occupation could still be seen. Here some of us disembarked to buy sugarcane, coconut, cocorite and other treats. The boat then steamed up river, with dolphins following, giving us a free performance to rival those at Sea World. Somewhere around 2 pm we knew that we were approaching Goshen when we were advised to collect our belongings and we could see pontoons navigated by an outboard motor leaving the shore coming towards the middle of the river. The speed of the boat was reduced and with the help of the sailors, we were safely deposited into the pontoons to be met by Brother John VanLange who tried to scare us from that first day, by regaling us with stories of the Kanaima who were so fierce that hair grew on their teeth.

Soon we were having a hearty supper prepared by Sister Brooks and her kitchen staff after we were assigned our units and captains within our divisions. We then met for evening worship, after which camp rules were explained and the next day's activities planned. Preparations for bed being made, a much needed rest was most welcomed.

Having so many campers posed a problem for religious services as we expected to be joined by church members from the area. The church which served the community was very small and situated near the bank of the river. The cabin built for the boys could not house them all, so it was decided that the unit with the oldest boys would be housed in the church. On that Friday, we all pitched in to create an amphitheater for the services of the weekend. We cut down trees and made benches and tied wild flowers with vines to the trees surrounding. It looked like hallowed ground was supposed to look; and when we started to sing among the trees, it was nothing short of heaven.

We behaved as good campers, doing our KP, arts and crafts, made up our bunk beds, passed inspection, observed rest periods, observed "lights out", and were punctual for all activities in order to have the points necessary to raise or lower the flag. There was such precision to our drills that the country's military could not hold a candle to us. At swim sessions, the girls and boys swam at different beaches, and all social activities were chaperoned to the fullest extent. Every evening after "lights out," the camp directors made rounds of the cabins and grounds. Nothing got past them except for one episode I know of.

Previously I mentioned that the unit of the oldest boys was housed in the church building near the water's edge. One night after "lights out" they decided to go for a swim. They were having quite a fine time when the "look out" caught a glimpse of a flashlight's beam in the distance. He whistled, and whispered in alarm, "The Professor" (affectionate name for Pastor Westney). Within a few seconds, the boys sped towards shore, shook the sand off their feet and jumped into their hammocks, covering their wet bodies with blankets. They were snoring so loudly that "The Professor" seemed satisfied when he flashed the beam of the flashlight; everything seemed to be in order. When he was out of earshot they collapsed in laughter for hours after; we giggled for a long time too when they told us.

Soon it was the night before we were to break camp and campers were scurrying around to secure addresses of those with whom they had become fast friends. We always had a special program for that night and many young people who had not yet been baptized, made the decision which was to be consummated on returning to their home churches. Tears were even shed and many friendships cemented since that time are still vibrant today after 55 years. One of my most significant friends from that era is Brenda Cozier Edwards, now residing in London.

When I was fifteen years old, the Mission (now a Conference) sponsored a trip to Kaieteur Falls and I was blessed to have a mother who was not afraid to have me broaden my horizons. We traveled from Wismar by boat, to Bartica by boat (2 days) then to Mahdia by truck, then over the Amatuk, then the Waratuk Falls, hiking and traveling every which way but flying, to get there. I remember shaking a few cracker crumbs into the river and the precision and swiftness with which the piranha attacked even the wrapping was awesome to behold. Shock from Electric Eels was a possibility in some of the rivers in which we swam.

When we beheld the majesty of the falls, it was all well worth it. The Kaiteur Falls has a drop of 741 feet which is four times as high as Niagara Falls. A glorious rainbow surrounds it when the sun is shining and it inspires awe just being in the vicinity.

On our way back down, when we arrived at Mahdia, we discovered that the truck's battery had lost its charge and we were obliged to wait for hours until a truck arrived from somewhere else to assist us. By this time our food supply was running low so another camper and I took a walk in the bushes to search for fruit, but instead we came across a man who offered us a piece of cassava (the Brazilian stick) which he cooked with some cod fish and fed us. I have never in my life before or since then tasted anything like it - flowery and sweet. We rejoined the group electing to leave that incident out of our report. Finally we headed for Bartica where we enjoyed indoor plumbing and good, hot food. We passed by Goshen on our way back home, humbled and enriched by our experience of viewing one of God's masterpieces.

THE WAY IT WAS

The devil was hard pressed to find work for our idle hands to do. Our parents made sure that we were not idle, at least not for too long. We awoke at 5:30am, had family morning devotions, did our chores such as preparing breakfast, milking the cow, stocking up the wood pile, fetching water from the creek, getting ready for school, eating breakfast and being at school before the bell rang at 8:30am. In addition I took piano lessons three days a week before school began. After school it was extra lessons for me in preparation for the Common Entrance exam, homework, fixing and eating supper, washing dishes, getting ready for the next day, evening worship then sleep.

On Sabbaths after church, if a church member happened to be hospitalized, we walked for miles, crossed the river, walked some more miles to visit the member and sing for the other patients in the ward. If no hospital visits were planned, we attended a Branch Sabbath school operated by my mother's cousin, Sister Stuger. Neighborhood children who did not attend any church were allowed to attend. Here's one of the songs we sang:

A is for Adam, who was the first man
B is for Bethlehem the place when Jesus was born
C is for Cain who killed his brother Abel
D is for Daniel who was cast in the Lion's den
E is for Enoch who was taken up into heaven
F is for the flood which drowned the world
G is for the giant Goliath who was slain by David
H is for Hannah who gave her son Samuel to the Lord
I is for Isaac the blessed man
J is for Jacob to whom an angel appeared in a dream
K is for Korah who was swallowed up by the earth
L is for Lazarus whom Jesus raised from the dead
M is for Methuselah the oldest man
N is for Nazareth, the place where Jesus lived
O is for Olivet the mount where Jesus prayed
P is for Pharaoh who was drowned in the Red Sea
Q is for the Queen of Sheba who visited King Solomon

R is for the Robe of Righteousness
S is for Solomon on the Throne of David
T is for Tiberius on the Sea of Galilee
U is for Uzza who steadied the Ark
V is for vine which represents Christ
W is for watchman on the walls of Zion
X is for Xerxes the King of Persia
Y is for yoke, the yoke of Christ
Z is for Zion, the home of the blessed

The Alphabet Song

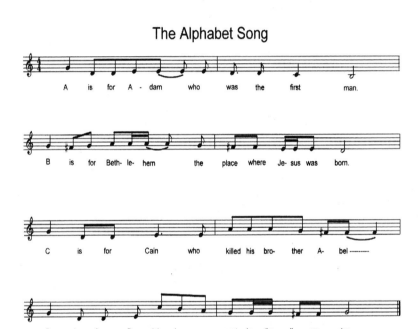

Music rewritten by
Jerry Cox

Once yearly the week of spiritual emphasis called the "Week of Prayer" was observed by members of all ages. The member who lived furthest away (Sister Bea) left home at 4am carrying a flambeau, or bottle torch, and as she approached the homes where other members lived, she called out and was joined by others carrying flashlights or lanterns, gathering a crowd as they went along. Approximately 70% of the residents at our end of Town belonged to one church or another hence the deduction "all the Christians live in Christianburg." By the time the group arrived at the church at 4:30am, we could see the members coming from the opposite direction. We, the children tried to find a comfortable pew to continue our naps but without success on account of the rapturous singing, praying, and the reading of the article.

Even as children we went home refreshed, running ahead of the grown ups, did our chores with zest and arrived at school really early. Years later the conference instituted a Youth's Week of Prayer which convened in the evenings. The blessing was the same. Children from those humble beginnings now reside in all of the West Indian Islands, the UK, the USA, Canada, Australia and beyond. When we meet or call each other, we still recall the way it was.

"YOU NEVER TO KNOW"

References:
1Sam. 16:7
Matt. 7:1 - 5
Luke 10:38 - 42
John 11:19 – 19

I lived in Trinidad in the 1960's, travelling to Port-of-Spain several times a month. It never failed; coming face to face with vendors of sweepstake tickets on the sidewalk. You couldn't escape them, they were everywhere, in front of Woolworth's, Glendining's, Salvatori building all around South Quay. They usually reminded you that "If you don't have a ticket, you don't have a chance," but there was this one fellow who tried to tip the decision scales in his favor by saying in a low monotone, "You never to know!"

On returning from Port-of-Spain, any question put to us was met with the answer "You never to know." We doubled over with laughter, imitating the fellow down to the slightest detail. Years later on studying the account of Mary and Martha entertaining Jesus, and Jesus raising Lazarus form the dead, I was forced to remark "You never to know!" In Luke 10:38 - 42, Jesus slightly chided Martha for being overly concerned with serving, at the same time complimenting Mary for sitting at His feet and listening to His words. We can assume that the dinner did go off without a hitch and that everything tasted quite right, but in her quiet moments, perhaps after the pottery was put away, she must have pondered these words, wondering how she might please Him.

Comparing that incident with the account of the death of Lazarus in John 11:19 - 29, it would seem that she was able to slip into the realm where she could hear from Jesus for herself. John recorded that both sisters were being consoled by friends in the house, but it was Martha (not Mary) who heard that Jesus was coming and went out to meet Him. Perhaps she was praying for that second chance and was ready when it came. The Bible says that "unto those that look for Him shall He appear that second time without sin into salvation." Heb.

66

9:28. After the preliminaries, the course of conversation changed to belief in the resurrection which Martha affirmed to be expected "at the last day." Then to her Jesus spoke those immortal words "I am the Resurrection and the Life..." These words were spoken to Martha over two thousand years ago and they resound until today at the home going of every saint, giving hope to the bereaved families.

Finally, Martha had come to know Jesus for herself. By looking at the outward appearance of a person, it is impossible to tell what deep down relationship exists between the person and God, therefore we are advised to defer judgment (Matt 7:1 -5). When the prophet Samuel was sent by God to the house of Jesse to anoint one of his sons as King, he was very impressed by the height, stature, bearing and countenance of David's seven brothers, but God reminded him "man looketh on the outward appearance, but the Lord looketh on the heart." 1 Sam. 16:7. We are to be concerned with our relationship to God, praying for others and speaking words of encouragement instead of magnifying the shortcoming of others who may be close to His heart as David was. After all "You never to know."

"AS I WAS WITH MOSES"

Reference Texts:
Josh. 1:5

After graduating from Caribbean Union College (now University of Southern Caribbean) in June of 1962 I was residing in the twin island nation of Trinidad and Tobago, waiting to begin my career. Excitement filled the air as the nation anticipated Independence from Great Britain after 160 years of British rule. There had been various competitions to choose a new national anthem, then music for the anthem, a flag and Independence Calypso King. Plans for the ceremony had to be fine tuned, flags and buntings and all the decorations made and installed as steel bands and militia bands practiced to perfection. Pre-Independence activities and excitement achieved a fevered pitch of frenzy that it was almost impossible not to get caught up in its grip.

The day chosen for the momentous occasion was August 31, 1962; the ceremony was scheduled to begin just before midnight on August 30th. Early in the afternoon my friend Henrietta and I along with her cousins wended our way to Frederick Street, then through Woodford Square, hoping to get as close as we could to the Red House. Arriving there as early as we did we found quite a good spot on Abercrombie St. between the square and the Red House.

A carnival atmosphere attended the crowd as we waited for hours for the ceremony to begin. It was impossible to ignore the conversations going on around as some denounced Jamaica for causing the failure of the Federation, others praised Dr. Eric Williams, older men recounted stories that they had heard from their parents about slavery, others talked about how good the British had treated the colonies, others disagreed, while some, wishing to be acknowledged, had definite ideas of how the new country should be run. The crowd broke out in peel of laughter and/or mutterings under breath (after all, this was Woodford Square). Vendors edged their way carefully through the crowd selling flags or food items as the excitement mounted. There were speculations ranging from what outfit the Queen's Representative would be wearing to which West Indian Island would be next to be granted Independence. There was a group of people to the right conversing in Patois. Ordinarily the English speaking people would have yelled, "Speak English" but not tonight, it was "Live and let live" in the congenial atmosphere.

At the time appointed the band began to play as the dignitaries and ceremony participants took their places. A hush fell, as everyone strained to listen, determined not to miss one word of the proceedings. As the ceremony proceeded, the time came when as the band solemnly played "God Save the Queen" for officially the last time and the Union Jack was lowered, the old men who had only a few hours before recounted hardship under the British, began to sob unashamedly. They continued crying even after the new flag was raised to the playing of the new National Anthem, "Forged from the love of Liberty in the fires of hope and prayer" and the thunderous roar of applause that followed.

At the end of the ceremony before dispersing, someone remarked to the men, "Boy, after all of your mouth, we didn't expect you to be bawling like a baby. What happened to you?"

The old men shook their heads and explained, "We knew what we had as bad as it might have been. We don't know what will be now, given the nature of man."

I supposed that Joshua felt the same way when he led the children of Israel over Jordan into the Promised Land after the death of Moses. God understood and encouraged him by saying to him "As I was with Moses, so I will be with thee. I will not fail thee nor forsake thee." And this He says to us when we encounter new stages in our lives such as going to a new school, moving to a new neighborhood or State, going into the hospital for procedures or any other unfamiliar events in life. Remember, as God was with Moses, Joshua, Abraham, Isaac, Jacob, your grandparents and your parents, He will be with you!

THE COW AND THE GIRAFFE

Reference Texts
Exod. 3:11
Job 38-41

Boys and girls! Today our story comes from nature and the God who made all things. In the Book of Job God asked Job questions concerning the foundation of the world, the heavenly bodies (constellations and stars) the wild beasts, the horses, the peacock, the lion, the ox, the eagle, the cow and many other works of His hands. These questions were asked of Job, not because he did not know the answers but as a recommendation to Him to trust the God who made all things. King Solomon said in Ecc. 3:11. He (God) hath made everything beautiful in his time.

Have you ever traveled in your family's car or with other friends and seen cows grazing contentedly in the meadows or even seen them on TV? The cows lower their heads to eat the grass on the ground after which they lie on the grass, chewing their cuds (ask you parents about this one). They never lift their heads any higher even when they "moo." In the winter they are fed in their stables with bales of hay, they never have to worry about where the grass or the hay is coming from. Nothing bothers a cow; she may even eat while being milked.

God has blessed me to visit Africa and one of the most amazing sights I saw in Kenya was the heads of five giraffes sticking out amount the trees all in one place. They were eating the leaves from the tree tops, just as effortlessly as ever. Not once did I see one of them lean over to eat some grass.

Then it occurred to me that God made every creature and placed their food within their reach. The giraffes did not have to bend over to eat the grass nor did the cow have to jump high to be fed from the tree tops. God fed everyone on his own level. Neither one had to change being what it was made to be in order to be fed.

God made us all uniquely with individual talents. No one is better than the other. We should not focus on changing the other person to our way of doing things, neither should we compare ourselves with others, talent wise, education wise or otherwise. The Bible says that comparing ourselves with each other is not wise. We would bring more glory to Him by pooling our talents together and working to improve our classes, our neighborhoods, and our world. Maybe one of you has a good singing voice or you may be able to read well and another is able to do sketches. You can get together and produce a dramatization of a Bible story for your Sabbath School class.

Remember that after every day of creation God said that His work was very good. Now ask your parents to sing with you or teach you the words to Hymn 93 "All Things Bright and Beautiful." Remember, no one is unimportant in God's eyes. Be yourself; He promises that every mouth will be fed.

HANDICAPPED? NOT ON YOUR LIFE!

Reference Texts:
Eccl. 4:9-12
Rom 12:4-8

Upon leaving the marketplace in Nairobi, Kenya, my friend and I were besieged on every side by beggars of all ages and compositions. There were little children, mothers with children, groups of teenagers, old people, all races and faces. Hunger was definitely offering equal opportunity to all. As we navigated our way through this maze, trying to get to the main street, we were thankful that our friends who were missionaries at the University of Eastern Africa at Baraton, had arranged for a native to escort us while in Nairobi.

Suddenly I saw an usually sight of a tall, well built man carrying a smaller, apparently crippled man on his back. The smaller man's legs were wrapped around the tall man's waist. They were weaving in an out of traffic with such agility that there was not enough time to assess their situation, having to watch the on-coming traffic which was about to run us over. I lost sight of the pair but I wondered about them several times that day. Being safely back at the Adventist school in Nairobi, we breathed a sigh of relief for having safely come through such traffic.

Later that day we journeyed to Eldoret, crossing the equator in the evening. We were disappointed that it was raining and dark when we crossed the boundary line and were unable to take a picture at the sign. That night around the fireplace as we recounted our experiences of the day my friends, Lydia and Newton, asked "By the way, did you see a tall, well built man carrying a cripple on his back?"

"As a matter of fact, I did! What's the story behind that? There was no time for me to assess the situation."

"The big tall man is blind," my friends informed me. "The cripple can see. The cripple navigates the blind man through traffic, directing him to areas where it is most likely that they would receive alms."

For a while I could not respond while pondering the ingenuity of these two handicapped persons who had figured out a way to pool their resources, talents and blessings for the nutritional benefit of them both. The blind man could not have lasted for five minutes in that Nairobi traffic coming from the airport. Neither would have the crippled man been able to move more than a few feet on his own, soon dying of starvation, given the competition.

Boys and girls, in life there are many setbacks and even handicaps, but instead of sulking over what we do not have, we need to offer what we have and we are sure to find someone who will offer what we need and together we can enjoy life much better than being alone. The Bible says "two are better than one" because they have a good reward for their labor (Eccl. 4:9). In the body of Christ we are all members although we are not given the same gifts and talents. Let us use whatever talents God has given us for the edifying of the whole body. Remember where there's a will there's a way!

A WAY OUT OF NO WAY

Reference Texts
Gen. 22:14
Prov. 3:6
Matt. 6:25 - 34

Girls and Boys do you believe that miracles still happen today? Well, they most certainly do! A great miracle was experienced within my family in the 1980s. One of my cousin's daughters was attending Boston University as a Pre-med student being well aware that had it not been for the Lord, she would not have made it that far. She had witnessed many smaller blessings such as the Banks making loans and even some Bank personnel made personal loans to her mother at the last minute so that she could pursue her goal of becoming a doctor. Since she was a little girl, she always knew that this was to be her life's work.

While in Boston she attended the Methodist Church from which our family originated. Not because she is my niece, but she always did have a humble and lovely spirit and was therefore assisting in the Sunday School and other activities. An interdenominational group of students met weekly for church services, socialization and exchange of information, and because of her willingness to assist in the preparation and tidying up of the area after the social activity, the church officers asked her about her family. She told them that her great-grandfather had been a Methodist Preacher at the turn of the 20th century in Guyana, and also her grandfather had followed the profession later on in his life. Pleasantries were exchanged and they looked forward to another social evening soon after.

On returning to classes that week she was horrified to discover that she needed to register for the next term by the following day or forfeit her place in class. Registration was open until the end of the next day and the fee was $2,500.00. In panic she called her mother, who was on the way to work the evening shift at the Dialysis Center several states away.

"Mom," she stuttered, "I won't be able to attend classes." "And," she added, "the registration fee is $2,500.00."

"2,500 what?," her mother asked in disbelief. "Child, I don't have 2500 cents," adding, "I'm on my way to work now, I can't think how I'm going to handle this one. We will do what we have always done and that is to pray." And with that being said, she decided how she would use her supper break.

She was assigned a supper break at 5pm, but instead of eating supper she went into the Chapel at the center and prayed. "Lord, this child is not mine. I gave her to you a long time ago. This problem is also not mine, but yours. If there's a way you want me to help you, please tell me how, but I know that you can do it." When her break was over, she returned to her unit, brainstorming as to what her next move should be.

At approximately 10pm, before her shift was over, she was paged for a phone call. Wondering at what the emergency could be, she was relieved to hear her daughter's voice at the other end of the line, but this time, there was excitement in her voice.

"Are you all right?" my cousin asked.

"Much more than all right, Mom. I am richly blessed. I was just awarded a Jessie Durrell scholarship for guess how much Mom? Can you guess? For exactly $2,500.00. I will be able to register for school after all."

Her mother, now flaberghasted asked, "And who is Jessie Durrell?" Her daughter tried to explain that Jessie Durrell was a person who had designated funds in his will for education of descendants of Methodist preachers in the New Hampshire (USA) district. That afternoon after the social, what she thought was just polite chatter, the information gathered was used to apply for the scholarship which she didn't even know existed. She was not informed that this was being done on her behalf because the clergymen did not know if she would have qualified for the scholarship being the 3rd generation from a Methodist preacher in Guyana. They did not want to raise her hopes in vain; but Papa Mac's (James McIntosh, my grandfather) work did follow him.

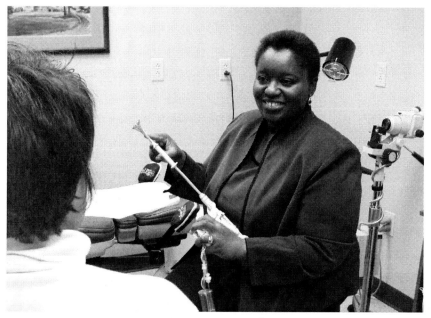

Dr. Denise A. Johnson

"Well, praise the Lord and thank Jessie Durrell" echoed her mother as she said her silent thanks to God who said that he would direct our paths if we acknowledge Him, taking no thought for the things we need. Remember girls and boys, as Abraham proved a long time ago "in the mount of the Lord it shall be seen."

Dr. Denise Johnson is now the Medical Director of a hospital in Pennsylvania.

FRIENDS INDEED

Reference Texts:
Prov. 17:17 & 18:24
Luke 7:34
James 2:23

There are many life lessons to be learned if only we would be observant. Last summer a pigeon became entrapped in an empty air conditioner sleeve towards the back of my house. On investigating the rapidly flapping sounds, I discovered that the back grill of the sleeve had collapsed inward cutting off its escape. What I also discovered was that three pigeons were perched on my neighbor's roof nearby. Occasionally one of them would fly off to return in a few minutes while another one would fly on to the sleeve, cooing, or whatever it is that pigeons do. Since I needed to wait for several hours for assistance to safely free the bird, I took the time to observe the interaction of the birds. The pigeon's friends never left him alone.

When help finally arrived, I donned a pair of gloves and oven mitts and pulled him safely into a plastic bag. I then walked him through the house in order to release him on the lawn, when I noticed, to my surprise, that the other pigeons had also walked across the roof to the front of the house. One of the pigeons was now perched on the eave of my house closely observing me, as if to say, "I'm here to see what you intend to do with my friend."

Even creatures have been created to show concern for each other as we learn from the ritualistic behavior of elephants when one of the herd is wounded or killed. Jesus is our example. He was accused of being a friend of the poor, the publicans and sinners. He never forsook his friends when they sinned.

In today's world it is possible that some of our friends could get into big trouble later on in life, and although it might not be a good idea to remain physically close to them, we can always be close to them in prayer. The Bible says that "a friend loveth at all times" even sticking closer than a brother. Jesus is your friend and brother who should be introduced to your earthly friends. Abraham was blessed to be called "the friend of God." How about you?

Entertaining A President Unawares

Reference Texts:
Gen. 19
1 Cor. 3:6
Heb. 13:2

"Young man, how would you like to attend our College?" was the question addressed to a first time visitor to our church at Wismar by my mother in March of 1962.

"Me, lady?" was the reply. "College? I am just an ordinary worker at the Bauxite Company and I've never attended High School. What would I be studying at college?"

"Who invited you to church? I've never seen you here before."

"I have been attending some meetings held by Sister Danny at Silvertown, where I live. She invited me to see how Communion is celebrated here at the Adventist Church."

"About college," my mother brought the conversation back to her point of focus, "come to my home tomorrow and I'll explain everything to you. I have a daughter over there right now. Anyone could direct you to my home. It's the first one after Katabuli Creek."

"Did I hear what I think I heard? Am I dreaming? Could this be really happening?" Hilton mused as he returned home after having lunch with a member of the church. He remembered thinking that God must have helped him to secure the job at the Bauxite Plant, a job he had actively pursued for three years. He also recalled how he had prayed at midnight in St. Adian's Anglican Church on New Year's Eve that God would change his life, not being quite sure what he meant by that.

Hilton wended his way to Christianburg with eager anticipation the following day. After explaining about dormitory life, educational courses and ensuing careers, my mother created a plan which would at least get him there some time in the following year. It was agreed upon that he would join the Box (Sou-Sou) she kept, at $20.00 per week. Hilton continued attending church for three out of four Sabbaths a month (he was obligated to work one Sabbath per mouth at the Plant).

He soon joined the choir conducted by Dennis Henry, also participating in all church activities. He enjoyed the Christian association with the other young people - Dick Hunter, Myrtle and Leonard Thomas, Bonnie Walton, Kenny Johnson, Uncle Bill Delapara, the Allicocks, the Charters, the Carryls, the Carrs and the McLennons, to name a few. Brother Hall was the church elder at that time. Hilton was sure of a place at my mother's table each Sabbath, along with anyone else who felt inclined to join her. All were welcome.

Hilton was experiencing problems at home because of the money for the box hand and the tithe. You see, before this, he never opened his pay envelope; he usually gave it to his mother. One of the brethren tried to make it easier for him by telling him that he did not have to tithe until he was baptized, but he was so consumed by what he had read in the Bible that he decided that if tithing was in the Bible, he would have to comply immediately.

Before my mother left for Trinidad to attend my graduation she told Hilton that it was time to write the application to the school. He confided to her that he did not know how to write an application, so she wrote it and took it with her. She made an appointment with the president of the College, B.G.O. French and on returning to Guyana; she informed him that he was expected to register for January 1963. This caused problems on the job since he was the youngest one there, and talking about going to College was rubbing the older men the wrong way.

Hilton gave up the job and was baptized on December 16, 1962 by Pastor Gordon who, as he baptized him, said prophetically, "Hilton, what I am doing to you today, you will be doing to others some day."

Before leaving for CUC he had a dream in which he saw Jesus with a lamb in his arms, surrounded by many sheep. Jesus said to him, "Take care of these."

Quite a few miracles were performed to get Hilton over to Trinidad. I remember my mother trying to scrape together the airfare. When Hilton left home, his family did not even say goodbye to him, so obviously, he was deserted as far as financial or emotional support was concerned. My mother sent him what she could, because by this time, she was also supporting a nephew and a son at college. He was given a placement test and enrolled in Form 2. This presented quite a challenge, being away from elementary school for 12 years. He worked in the kitchen as a dishwasher, studied hard every night, and was encouraged by being taken along to Prayer Band by Brother Kirk (a fellow student) after study period.

Dr. Hilton Garnett

He learned the art of becoming a Literature Evangelist, canvassing in San Fernando, Trinidad, Tobago, St. Kitts, Linden, Guyana and in 1964 on his way to St. Kitts, when the boat stopped in St. Lucia, he received the devastating news of my mother's death from a terrorist bomb placed ion the boat in which she and many others were traveling. Our church lost five members that day. Hilton completed his secondary education, entered the Ministerial Program and graduated in 1968 with honors.

Pastor Garnett subsequently continued his education in Jamaica from 1975 to 1977, returning to Guyana as Personal Ministry Director, the position he held until he left for Andrews University in 1981, to return in 1983 with a Masters Degree. His mother, who passed in 1984, lived long enough to be proud of his accomplishments. In 1985, Pastor Garnett was called to be the Secretary of the East Caribbean Conference, returning to Guyana as Conference President in January of 1990. After two terms as President, he left for Canada where he resided for 11 years, where he held the position of Ministerial Director of the Ontario Conference for four years.

Pastor Garnett returned to Guyana in April of 2007 as Conference President for the second time. This time he returned as Dr. Hilton Garnett with a Doctorate in Ministry and Christian Counseling. He is the spiritual leader of over 50,000 believers, from a total of 175 congregations. This year 2008 marks his 40th year in ministry. In addition to soul winning, his goals include an aggressive agenda to foster health screening (a mobile unit has just recently arrived in the country) and plans for a senior citizen's home are also afoot. He has been blessed, along with his wife, to have three children who are making their mark in the world: a son holding a doctorate in Microbiology and Genetics, a daughter who holds a Master's Degree in Sociology and a daughter with a Master's Degree in Special Education from Johns Hopkins University. Look at what the Lord had done!

To agree with the Apostle Paul, Sister Danny planted, my mother watered, and God certainly gave the increase. Blessed be the name of the Lord!

Georgiana "Mammy" Hinds

DADDY'S GIRL

Reference Texts:
Zech. 2:8

You haven't met a doting father if you didn't know Samuel Nathaniel Hinds, native of Barbados. He always knew what he wanted and protected those he loved. I'm told that at the engagement party he was already passing out the printed invitations for the wedding for the marriage to my mother in 1939. When I arrived almost five years later, he could not be contained and he let everybody know it. The people who did not live in our neighborhood thought that he was a widower because everywhere they saw him, there was this little girl perched on this shoulders as if she could not walk, or that he had no one to leave her at home with.

I can remember everything that happened to me from the age of three. I can remember that the only Sabbath he stayed home from services was the time that I contracted the measles. He told me to point to the spot that itched, and he gently rubbed the area with a soft towel. My father liked to cook. At the drop of a hat he would have a coconut grated and potatoes sliced, rice washed, onions diced and a good stew in progress. I can still vividly recall seeing his favorite pot which he soldered when it became cracked. Quite obviously, my mother fed me before I went to sleep, but if he came home at midnight he would cook and wake me up to feed me. I can remember falling asleep on myself trying to chew the food.

He devised all sorts of games for us to play. Although he named me Vashti, yet in some of the plays I was Queen Esther (he was going to have a Queen one way or the other). He made me a stool, which was my throne, he made me a crown out of rolling one of my mother's stockings, and the long stem from the papaw tree was my scepter. He would approach the throne and if I did not hold out my scepter, he could not come any closer. My mother used to rebuke him, "Sam, I've never seen a father to dote on a child as much as you do." When sugarcane was in season, he would cut the wedges just the right size for my mouth, placing the trash can within reach. He bought us a gramophone which he spent hours playing (the only one in the neighborhood). I remember that one of the tunes was composed of the words of Psa 27:4 "One thing have I desired of the Lord, and that will I seek after."

I remember that his mother passed some time between my 3rd and 4th birthdays, my brother had just been born, my mother remained at home, so I had my daddy all to myself. In those days an old African tradition was observed at funerals in British Guiana; young children were passed over the casket by the relatives to be received by relatives on the other side. I asked him lots of questions about the casket and this is what he told me: "When Jesus comes, the casket will break open and you'll see Mammy. She won't be sick or anything, so don't worry about crying or anything. You'll miss her, but it won't be for long." I did not cry as I saw the older ones doing because, if my Daddy said it would be so, it would be so. After the funeral, I remember him taking me to the Botanical Gardens to feed the Manatee and picking one of the flowers (forbidden) to place in my hair.

When my brother came along I could no longer ride on his shoulders, but then he held my hand and carried my brother. When my brother grew, he held us each by the hand. My cousin, Cynthia, an octogenarian still reminds me of seeing him in the distance coming to visit them holding both of us by the hand. I soon began attending kindergarten at Brother Miller's Pilgrim Holiness Church School. I missed spending so much time with him, but it was not unusual for him to stop by the school to make certain that I was all right. By this time he was employed on a building project at Mackenzie. He traveled to work by himself in a row boat (Ballahoo).

Early one Sunday morning in August 1950, he woke me, asking me if I would like to go to New Amersterdam with our tenant. Of course I was excited to go, but disappointed that he would not be going along. He gave me a shiny silver sixpence (12 cents) as my vacation spending money, took me to the stelling to catch the streamer, and hugged and kissed me goodbye. We were supposed to visit for a week; I was told that there were children at the house in New Amersterdam.

We stayed overnight in Georgetown and early that Monday morning we caught the train to Rosignol. It was quite an adventure for me seeing the telegraph poles whizzing by, the neat vegetable gardens, the cows and donkeys in the meadows, recognizing the different sounds as the train passed over creeks and trenches, and the bustle when the train chugged into the stations. The hissing and roaring of the big black steam engines puffing billows of black smoke was quite foreboding at first, but I soon learned to love the smell of the smoke and the blast of the whistle. At Rosignol we took the ferry across the Berbice River to New Amersterdam, and then a taxi to the house.

I played with the children for the rest of that day and all of the next day Tuesday. Even as a little child just barely six years old I was attuned to what was happening around me. I remember that the top tune at the time was "Caledonia, Caledonia, what makes your big head so hard?"

About mid morning on Wednesday I remember a man coming to the door and being told, after he left, that we would have to pack our things to return home. Although I was disappointed at not spending the entire week as we were supposed to, this meant that I would be seeing my Daddy so much the sooner. We took the taxi to the ferry, the ferry to the train and when the train stopped at Mahaicony, where vendors sold all sorts of food items like fish and bread, channa, custard blocks, mittai, salara, pineapple tarts, fruits in season, vegetables and seasonings, I bought five mangoes for a bit and pocketed my change of 2 big copper pennies (4 cents).

On arriving at the stelling on Thursday morning to board the steamer for Mackenzie, I was surprised to see all of my cousins from both sides of my family also boarding the boat. I was overjoyed at seeing them all which engendered visions of happy and long hours of playtime. "Are you also coming to our house?" I asked one of my father's nieces.

Excitedly and innocently Eunice blurted out "Don't you know that your father drowned?"

"My father? Are you sure? When? How did it happen?"

She told me what she heard and immediately there was a peace in my heart because I remembered what he had told me when his mother passed.

When we got to our house my mother was looking out of the bedroom window near the rubber tree and she was sobbing. I went to her and said, "Don't cry, I have money" producing the two pennies. She gently caressed my face and dried her eyes for my benefit. Everyone was observing me closely but not directly, expecting an outburst of some kind which never came. I then went to the place where he hung his work clothes to figure out what he was wearing: a pair of pinstripe, navy trousers and a blue shirt were missing.

I remember the "Ranger" (the boat used by the Commissary) towing his body when it was discovered on Friday after which there was a quickly organized service. Some of his sisters fainted, someone gave me some flowers, and the church folks sang "In the Land of Fadeless Day" while Sister Andrews was holding David who had no idea of what was going on; then it was over. Of course my mother and all the relatives were at church the next day, people speaking in hushed tones when I approached.

My mother recounted that they had separated after morning worship, he went to work in his boat and she went to the Post Office after leaving David at the neighbor's. A heavy fog usually enveloped the river early in the morning, then dissipated when the sun came up. A large ship, called the "London Mariner," loaded with bauxite being transported to Canada, left the pier in the fog with the tide being low. The ship, being so heavily laden, became stuck on the sand bank and in trying to maneuver itself out of its predicament, caused excessive waves which capsized my father's boat. The caretaker at the Rest House saw the accident and literally ran to the Post Office (she had seen my mother go by) and calling her outside said, "Sister Hinds, don't mail that money to your sister, you will need it yourself." She then recounted what she had seen. Later on an inquest was held and a law was passed that the ships could not leave the docks until the fog cleared. This is the hymn sung by my father during morning worship that day, August 23, 1950:

Thy way not mine, O Lord,
However dark it be
Lead me by thine own hand
Choose thou the path for me.

I dare not choose my lot
I would not if I might
Choose thou for me my God,
So shall I walk aright.

The kingdom that I seek
Is thine so let the way
That leads to it be thine
Else I must stray

Hold thou my cup of life
With joy or sorrow fill
As best to thee may seem
Choose thou my good and ill

Choose thou for me my friend
My sickness or my health
Choose thou my cares for me
My poverty or wealth.

Not mine, not mine the choice
In all things great and small
Be though my guide, my strength
My wisdom and my all.
Horatius Boner

This is the only photograph I have of my father or of our family together. I was about four and a half years old when my Dad came home excitedly telling my mother to get us dressed in a hurry because Elder Dirgoo (affectionately so called) who was in charge of all Literature Evangelists was coming to the house in a few minutes with a camera. I remember when the picture was taken and by whom. Prints were shared out among family members until eventually, the last one disappeared. When I lost my mother almost seventeen years later, my thoughts went back to this picture as being the only one of the whole family. At the time I was living in San Fernando, Trinidad and when it occurred to me that Elder Dirgoonanan was then retired and living in Cocoyea Village, although I knew it was rather a very long shot, I decided to pay him a visit. I introduced myself and reminded him of my father. Immediately his face lit up and I made my request. He said, "Give me a week, let me see what I can do."

When I returned after a week, good old Elder Dirgoo presented me with the negative; imagine after seventeen years! I was then able to have prints made and again distributed to the younger relatives, including my brother, who was not blessed to know much about my father in this life. I cannot fully imagine what God means when He says that we are "the apple of his eye," but I came pretty close, because beyond the shadow of a doubt, I was the apple of my Daddy's eye." I was 1000% Daddy's girl!

NEVER AN ILL WIND BLOWS

Reference Texts:
Rom. 11:33

This story needs to be told, but as delicately as possible, so that the gory details are omitted. Race relations in British Guiana were exemplary while I was growing up, an occasional outburst between African and East Indian descendants was soon quelled, onlookers actually telling the participants that they should be ashamed of themselves. All of this changed in 1963 initiated by an 80-day general strike, which led to rioting and general break down of law and order. The two leading political parties - PPP led by Cheddi Jagan and the PNC

Winifred Hinds-Giles

led by L.F.S. Burnham - divided the country in allegiance, pitting the East Indians and African descendants against each other. Soon vicious crimes, such as burning of homes and equally retaliatory immoral and illegal acts were being committed by both groups. To escape being burned alive our East Indian neighbors often found refuge at nights in our home because of my mother's standing in the community.

On July 6th, 1964, while traveling from Georgetown to Linden on the "Sun Chapman," through a politically engineered terrorist attack, my mother, along with many others, lost her life. Our church lost five members in that one day. I can only imagine the impact, since I was a nursing student in Trinidad at that time. A state of emergency was declared which meant that no airplanes were allowed in or out of the country. When the news of the attack reached Linden, it spawned a new wave of rioting and other atrocities. Some time later when communication was restored, my relatives and life long family friend Dennis Henry provided the sad details. In my grief and anguish I could still see the kindness of God on my behalf allowing me to remember her the way she was when she attended my graduation in 1962.

Not realizing how much the country's system had deteriorated. I had planned to visit British Guiana in June of that year, but postponed the trip to wait for my brother to accompany me in August, since we had not been at home together in years,. This incident occurred in July, fourteen years after my father's accident in the same river and fourteen miles apart in location.

My anguish was put on the back burner when I was informed that one of the church members who also perished, Sister Carmen Carryl, was the mother of seven children, six boys and one girl, the youngest being a boy of 18 months, all of them much younger than we were. This was a lady I knew well, I knew her mother, her sister, her brothers and her nephew was a former classmate of mine. I forgot my own troubles and turned to praying for them. I was already employed and would try to take care of my brother and cousin who were at the boarding school, but the very thought of a man being left to raise seven children without

Sister Edna Dublin who also perished in the "Sun Chapman" Tragedy

any time for him to even grieve properly, was very overwhelming to say the very least. As the years went by I inquired of their welfare and continued praying for them whenever the thought of the family entered my mind.

God's blessings attended and there were no delinquents among those children. To crown it all, the 18 month old boy grew up to become one of Brooklyn's top surgeons, having distinguished titles as Chairman of the Department of Surgery and Director of the Surgery Residency Program at one of the leading hospitals in the Borough. He also returns to Guyana every year, also visiting other West Indian islands and parts of South

Africa to provide free medical aid. My satisfaction was realized when my brother, who is now a Physician's Assistant was able to accompany him on one such visit to Guyana. Our mothers would have been well pleased.

As Caribbean school children many of us detested having to learn "Parables." One such parable that did not make any sense to me was, "It's an ill wind that blows nobody any good." I could not for the life of me see its connections to anything that was going on around me, until years later. Another benefit derived from this experience, was that it enabled me to identify with the families of the September 11 victims with whom I came in contact, especially those caring for the children left behind. I was able to tell them that I know a God who did wonders for a man with seven children and that He could do it for them. A perfect family does not always consist of both parents, but if God is the Father we cannot help but turn out perfectly. In Paul's epistle to the Romans he says, "O the depth of the riches both of the wisdom and knowledge of God! How unsearchable are his judgments and his ways past finding out!" Rom. 11:33.

Stephen S. Carryl, M.D., FACS

My Grandparents
Flora Griffith McIntosh (Born 1882)
James McIntosh (Born 1880)

"Meet Our Golden girls...and Boys"

The McIntosh family has always been close knit. Memories are still fresh in my mind of the days when we spent our school vacations and Christmases together at Aunt Julie's (our great aunt) home in Mahaica (she was a nurse at the Sanitarium). One of the sisters would do all the baths, another would braid the hair (the style at the time was the "upsweep"), while another would prepare the clothing or have the meal ready. As children we could not contain ourselves, anxiously anticipating the train ride. In those days family members (children and all) showed up to "spend time." We as children, were delighted because we were left to play for hours while the grown up talked. Children dared not be in the house during adult conversation; having and stating an opinion was a death sentence. We are still carrying on our tradition. We hold family reunions, every wedding or funeral is a reunion, we speak to each other several times weekly or daily and all the children belong to us and we belong to the McIntosh sisters. Now, meet them in order of birth.

Uncle Fred was a teacher whom very few of us remember. He took his vocation very seriously, visiting homes to inquire about children who were absent from school. In those days the salary for a teacher was $12.00 per month, from which rent was paid, a family was maintained and the teacher was expected to be well suited everyday. He taught principles of hygiene to us, the older ones, but he passed from this life at a very early age after a surgical intervention. The family felt this loss keenly. Who knows what else he could have accomplished, given his love for education?

My mother, Winifred, was next. Much is said about her throughout the book, therefore this would be a brief paragraph. Her sisters still remember how as teenagers, she taught them every new song she learned, as she gathered them around the table at nights. She loved singing, willingly providing the special music for church services each week. Her sisters recall how her wedding was a village affair, with villagers bringing eggs for the cake until Mama was constrained to refuse further donations. The baker designated a day in which he would be baking her cake only; all other orders were reassigned to another day. The sisters spread white sheets for her to walk on from the house to the car. She had such a great sense of humor. One night at evening worship my brother was designated to find and read a Psalm; and being sleepy, I guess, he chose Psalm 117 (having 2 verses). My mother said, "Boy, you'd better find another one on your own, or else I'll have you to read Psalm 119 (176 verses). Of course we all laughed at that.

Undoubtedly, she was a great woman of prayer, but there was one section of her daily prayer which perplexed me. She used to pray "Lord please give me health and strength." To me, this prayer was downright redundant because I figured that strength naturally followed health or was a component thereof. Boy was I wrong! The longer I live, I'm finding out that "it ain't necessarily so."

She was young at heart; most of the young people at the church congregated at our house. Strangers to the area eventually found themselves at our house and all were welcome. From those humble beginnings she has achieved worldwide recognition. To her credit, belongs the author of this book, who, on completing a Master's Degree in Community Health from Long Island University, pursued a Management Nursing career until retirement; her son David Hinds, who is a Physician's Assistant serving in many facilities in rural North Carolina; grandson Sheldon K. Andrews, an accomplished Graphic Designer responsible for all the illustration in this book, including the cover. David's children, Imari and Bakara are still young and have not decided on careers, but Bakara is leaning towards a performance and musical career. She is also claimed by a host of spiritual sons and daughters serving the Lord around the world.

Uncle James was named after my grandfather. He lived mostly in the interior of the country, referred to as the Gold Fields. His visits to the family home were far and in between, but I remember that when he did come home, there were 100 lbs bags of flour, sugar, rice and candy and snacks for us. He also maintained a couple of supply stores in the North West District. We did not see as much of him as we would have liked, but we knew that he was part of the family. His children are involved in the Family Reunion.

Aunt Beulah, as I was made to understand, was trained at Carnegie Home Economics School and was employed at the YMCA as a caterer. I am told that when she began her job she excitedly told her sisters of a beautiful hat which she was planning to buy with her first paycheck. She was unaware that the conversation was being overheard by my grandmother who interjected "Young lady, just be sure that your paycheck is enough to buy hats for all of your sisters." It was the custom in my family that the first paycheck was to be shared with the family and the poor. Aunt Beulah suffered a stroke when I nine years old, my mother took responsibility for two of the four children, the toddler was sent to live with Aunt Julie, then retired, with whom the eldest child

Constance was already residing. In those days there was not much in the way of Physical Therapy, so it was a miracle that she recovered enough to regain her speech, ambulation and coordination to be employed by the Bauxite Company at Ituni Hospital. The day my mother took her out of the hospital where it was apparent that she was not receiving any care (my mother dressed her and left a note on the bed and brought her home) although she could not speak, she was so happy to see that I was already cooking meals, that she communicated to me how proud she was of me. Three of her four children are registered nurses, the eldest, Constance achieving the status of Ward Sister before immigration to the USA. Aunt Beulah was blessed to retire from her job and join her children in the USA, beating the odds to live more than fifty years after her initial stroke. She lived to the ripe old age of 89, departing this life on July 6, 2006, exactly 42 years (to date) after her beloved sister.

Meet Aunt Mildred, chorister and dancer of the Golden Girls. Being mother of eight children (one deceased) she was very resourceful. I well remember how she saved the day when my mother remarried. Our outfits were bought well in advance, so that my brother had already outgrown his shoes by the time of the wedding. Imagine the consternation - a ring bearer without shoes. My Aunt said to my mother "I'll be right back.." She had dressed and taken her children to the church and had returned to assist us. She went back to the church where her son, Elton, had fallen asleep in the pew, gently eased his shoes off his feet and brought them for my brother to wear. They fit perfectly. When I lived in her home while attending High School our homework included learning the 24 rules of etiquette from a book by Emily Post (I think). There is one rule that still resounds in my memory today - "Speak quietly and courteously; quiet speech is a mark of refinement."

She possessed a most sweetly distinguishable voice heard in any congregation. I remember telling my friends that when she sang, you could hear all the other parts(alto, tenor, bass) blending in. (So much for prejudice) She always seemed to know when one of us (her nieces) was going through a difficult time and before long we would receive a letter/telegram with sometimes as little as four words. My last telegram read "Be still and know." She showed up to visit unexpectedly at any time. Her visits were always the highlight of our lives; re-telling stories of the family for as far back as she could remember.

She always liked the finer things of life so she subsequently joined the "Toastmistress Club" of Guyana, traveling to several islands and eventually to the USA, where she obtained employment to assist her children and grandchildren to realize their ambitions. To her credit many of her grandchildren have excelled in the medical field - a Sister Tutor, and OB/GYN doctor who was President of the Medical & Dental staff when the hospital where she is employed received the Premier Award for Excellence two years in a row, also chief of OB/GYN; a PhD majoring in Journalism, who interviewed a former US President; a Psychologist; several nurses and other careers equally as satisfying.

At the age of 85 she traveled unaccompanied to Nigeria and returned to spearhead a drive to supply wheelchairs to persons crippled by polio in the area she visited. The party really got started when she arrived and at 86 she was still doing the "electric slide". She encouraged us to trust God through seemingly difficult times. She was one of a kind!

Aunts Mildred, Beryl, Beulah and Elaine

Aunt Beryl turns 87 today as I write. I concluded a call to her in Guyana only a few minutes ago; where she was being assisted by her granddaughter to cook for her neighbors, friends, church members and children, all visiting ,along with the Pastor, to celebrate with her. She always possessed a quiet strength and approached life with optimism.

She contributed significantly and sacrificially to our education regardless of whose child needed assistance. She relinquished her bicycle to me when I started to attend High School although she really needed it at the time as a student midwife. As children we looked forward to her visits, she brought us the latest in snacks, eg. "Brown Betty" ice cream and Cracker Jack. She walked for miles to bring me dolls. She taught me to knit sweaters and socks and to smock my dolls' dresses. In those days the knitting needles used were in reality pointers from the coconut broom and the yarn was the twine ripped out of flour bags. She remembered our birthdays and wrote to the Radio Station requesting special songs like "The Teddybear's Picnic."

As a midwife she delivered over four thousand babies during her career. One outstanding pre-mature infant weighed less than 2 lbs; moving him to the town would have been detrimental, so she found ingenious ways to beat the odds. She wrapped him in thick flannel, nursed him in a shoe box to conserve his body heat, fed him with a medicine dropper. Today he is a grandfather.

She travels to the USA for family reunions, weddings and funerals, but she prefers to live in Guyana. When she visits she is sure to return with barrels of clothing for the less fortunate on her island home in the Essequibo River. Many of the babies she delivered, who are now adults residing in the USA feel honored to have her visit with them for a few days; they think of her as family, not merely as "Nurse". She has also written many poems which should still be published. She still plants a vegetable garden and travels unaccompanied, walking for miles. God bless you as you have blessed others and "Happy Birthday to you!"

Last, but certainly not least is Aunt Elaine, who is the most prolific of all the McIntosh clan. She is the mother of eleven children (one deceased) and is in her 85th year of life. I'm told that being the baby of the family, she was upset when Mama gave two biscuits to the others for snacks and gave her only one. Although not a psychologist, my grandmother solved the problem by taking the biscuit from her and, while Aunt Elaine was distracted , broke it into two halves then returned them to her, at which she was very pleased because now she had two biscuits as the big girls had. She has always been soft spoken, but having had eleven children, one can be sure that she has endured her share of trials and tribulations. For most of her life, she resided in the Pomeroon district in Essequibo County. She has produced two Pastors, teachers, a captain, and a host of other meaningful career holders. One of her granddaughters typed 80% of the manuscript for this book; she is also employed as an Engineering Designer in Construction Management at one of New York City's energy supply companies. Another grandson is presently in Medical School in Cuba. She enjoys returning to Guyana to visit her children and grandchildren.

Although not a McIntosh by birth, this chapter would be incomplete without the mention of my step father, Harry Giles affectionately called Uncle Harry or Bruds by the community. He was a very humorous character and there are certain phrases that were unique to him, for instance if someone should ask him, "Uncle Harry, why did John do such and such?", his reply would be simply "He knows." On Fridays he would clean all our shoes for church and would wash all the dishes on Saturday nights, giving us a longer time to interact with our friends after MV meeting. Our home was always filled with young people from the church, and a portion of our home was rented out to another family which included teenagers; then at one time there were "The boy in the barrel," his sister and mother: Sister Mat, Elaine and Noel Moses; there was never a dull moment at our home. At nights it was a comedy trying to fall asleep because we talked and giggled back and forth over the partition. One night Uncle Harry really wanted to get to bed early, but the laughter was contagious and uncontrollable. Exasperated he called out "Vashti, David, Joseph, Daphne, Ezme, Leonard, Myrtle, Darrell."

"Yes, Da."
"Yes, Bruds."

"You are all scholars", he continued. "Let me see which one of you can tell me what this abbreviation means. T.T.S."

"Take time slowly," was on offering.

"Two timing snake" was another suggestion

Finally we chorused "We give up Bruds, what is it?"

"Time to sleep," he declared and laughter broke out all over again, not subsiding for quite some time. My mother said "You should know better, Harry, you know that this would just start them up. You know is does not take much."

Until this day when we speak to each other at nights we end the conversation by saying, "I guess its T.T.S."

He also rescued me from a lot of manual discussion (whipping) by my mother. I would run when she tried to catch me, but I would be sure to run up into the guava tree where I would have something to eat until he came home to arrange my reprieve. He knew that I liked peanut butter, so he would slip me a jar for me to keep in my room.

Uncle Harry

He was an easy sale for anything from ice to insurance and he always had a good reason for buying the things he did. He was a good soul, who had a great relationship with others. Helping older people and family members came naturally to him.

Another positive male role model within the family was Aunt Mildred's husband, J.B. London. I lived within their household during my last four years of High School at which time they were the parents of six children all of whom were younger than I was. He was a master of many trades among which were the trades of blacksmith, wheelwright, joiner, building contractor. He was also the village chairman for a number of years and a lay preacher of the Methodist Church with special dispensation to administer sacraments in the absence of an ordained minister

I remember well, when I was much younger, that my mother considered reconstruction of our house, Uncle Joseph was obviously the contractor of choice for the job. He journeyed from the East Coast of Demerara to Christianburg (a full day's journey) intending to stay until the job was finished. He brought with him two apprentices whom he taught the trade, inspecting everything they did, and to top it all, at nights he saw to it that they wrote letters to their families back home, correcting any mistakes in the letters before they were mailed. They

Uncle Joseph and Aunt Mildred

were also required to read aloud at nights, do their own laundry and to ask his permission for everything they wanted to do.

As a blacksmith and wheelwright he was contracted by the adjoining sugar estates Lusignan and Non Pariell to shoe the mules and horses; the locals also brought donkeys to be fitted. I became acquainted with tools such as the hammer, the anvil, the bellows and the distinctive smell of blacksmith's coals which is different from ordinary coals. It was mesmerizing to see how effortlessly he made the horseshoes, hearing the hissing of the hot iron in the water. We took turns working the bellows and seeing how easy it seemed to be, Jean, Ingrid and

I decided to make horseshoes. What emerged, for all our effort, was a pitiful caricature.

As village chairman, many village elders unceremoniously dropped in to discuss village matters and the effects these matters were having on them. During the mango season, the villagers brought buckets of mangoes for us. I recall many nights, especially moon lit ones, that we would wash a whole bucket of mangoes, picking out the best (the not-so-good-ones went to the animals) sitting on the steps near the calabash trees, enjoying them to the fullest, with the juice running down to our elbows.

He was everybody's Uncle Joseph in the extended families that even his children called him "Uncle Joseph" from hearing the rest of us addressing him. He encouraged all children, he was gentle and had a humorous chuckle and ensuing laugh. He was very caring of Grandmother (his mother) when she came to harvest calabashes. That day turned out to be like a picnic. It was no wonder that his last daughter became Guyana's Sports Woman of the Year in 1979 competing in swimming in Russia and parts of the Caribbean. He also found time to plant vegetables, installing an irrigation system for easier watering of the garden. He took his religious vocation very seriously and could always be found helping others by advice or in action.

This is my great Aunt Juliet Roach, at whose home we all met as children, when the school year ended. The experiences were so unforgettable that we formed our North American Branch of the McIntosh Family Reunion which is a biannual affair. We wanted our children to experience the joy of family that still holds us together today. Aunt Julie was a nurse at the Leprosarium in Mahaica, returning to live in Buxton after retirement.

Aunt Juliet

Other great aunts and uncles included Uncle Alec, who lived to be 100 years old, Aunts Florrie, Eva, Dorothy, May and Carrie, who were loved for their individual characteristics.

MY BROTHER, DAVID.

Now just a few words about my brother, David Hinds. I was always very protective of him, maybe subconsciously because he was not old enough to know my father very well. I remember taking him to our older cousin's house to hide him instead of taking him to school, because we were told that the school nurse was going to visit the following day. To me the school nurse's visit portended vaccinations and I was determined to protect him from the sting of the needle.

I told my cousin that David was not feeling well and that my mother was working, so she gladly obliged. It was the mercy of God that no vaccinations were administered that day or he would have been unprotected from whatever disease the vaccination would have been against.

David had a dry sense of humor growing up. One day he was swimming in the river when it began to rain. He immediately ran out of the river to everyone's amazement. When asked the reason for so doing, he replied "Gosh, I don't want to get wet."

When I was just beginning to learn to cook, I thought that I was giving David a treat by making his favorite for dinner - rice porridge. I guess that the consistency was not quite right so he innocently asked "Vashti, where is the stew for this rice?"

Just as close as I was to my father, he was as close to my mother, so that I felt her loss more keenly for him than for myself. When I was ready to immigrate to the USA, David wanted to remain in Guyana to work at the Davis Memorial Hospital, but I would not hear of it. I just could not bear the thought of being so far away from him, not being sure whether he was being cared for. I mustered up the passage and we both traveled to New York together. When he joined the US Army, I cried to break my heart. He was always military/medically minded. Together with my cousin, Joseph Daniels, he started the Medical Cadet Corp while on the campus of Caribbean Union College in 1965. Here is a picture of him as Commander inspecting the Corp with Desmond

Doss, the only conscientious objector to receive a Medal of Honor from the US for his bravery in WWII.

I have told David how much like our father he is, always busy, taking advantage of business opportunities and making time for his children. David looks like him, walks like him, smiles and knits his brow like my daddy. So much for DNA. I pray for the day when our family will be reunited and they will have the pleasure of each other's company.

References

A Book of Narrative Verse
Published by Geoffrey Cumberledge
Compiled by VH Collins
Oxford University Press

Black Water People
By, Carmen Barclay Subryan

Guyana-Fraudulent Revolution
Published by Latin America Bureau

Holy Bible-King James Version

Nelson's West Indian Reader
By, J.O. Cutteridge

GLOSSARY

Bakes   Mixture of flour, water, salt, yeast or baking powder; coconut milk or shredded coconut, may also be added. Bakes are usually fried, roasted or baked. Enjoyed with cod fish and is usually a breakfast item

Ballahoo   Flat-bottomed wooden row boat.

Bellows   Instrument made of pleated leather attached to a handle, used by a blacksmith to fan coals into flame.

Calabash   Green gourd which when sawed open can be used for making household articles and purses.

Cassava Bread Flat bread made from dried cassava flour, baked within a metal hoop on baking pan. Dried in the sun, usually on zinc sheets. Sweet Cassava Bread-stewed grated coconut encased in a smaller hoop sandwiched between two small cassava breads.

Channa   Chick peas boiled and seasoned with salt, pepper and onions.

Chiggers   Larvae of blood-sucking mites, found on the toes of persons who walk barefooted in certain soils. The area of infection becomes swollen and irritated. Causes fever.

Chocolate	Sticks made from roasted cocoa beans, grounded and rolled into sticks. Makes a delicious breakfast beverage usually boiled with bay leaves and cinnamon sticks, milk and sugar added.
Corial	canoe carved out of a tree trunk.
Custard Block	Squares of frozen custard, frozen in ice trays.
Folklore	**Bush Dai Dai**-evil spirit of the forest. **Kanaima** - fierce tribe similar to the Arawak, reputed to having hair growing on teeth (told to scare children). **Massacuraman (male) & Water Mooma (female)** - hideous creatures reputed to inhabit rivers, snatching un-suspecting humans, especially children.
Fruits	**Cocorite** - brownish fruit of a palm tree, grows in bunches; has a large brown seed. **Coriyo** - greenish fruit of a palm tree, grows in bunches sometimes the skin turns yellow. Has large black seed. **Granadilla** - Barbadine (Trinidad & Tobago) fruit, size of a melon, the inside of which looks like and tastes like a passion fruit. Grows on a vine, has greenish yellowish skin. **Guava** – luscious small round fruit with small edible seeds. Comes in various varieties. **Jamoon** - small, dark, maroon colored fruit, size of a cherry, grows in bunches used to make wine. Stains clothing. **Locust** – brownish hairy substance covering black seeds in a brown pod. Not very palatable: locally called "stinking toe." **Malacca** – Pomerac (Trinidad & Tobago) red pear shaped fruit, with large seed surrounded by whitish flesh, consistency of an apple. **Mammy** – fruit the size of a cantaloupe, with thick

rough brown skin, yellow and pulpy flesh, seeds large brown and rough.

Mango – fruit originating in India of many varieties and flavors. Can be eaten fresh or dried and is an invaluable ingredient in many desserts and skin preparations.

Sour Sop – greenish, elongated, heart shaped fruit with soft spikes. Fruit inside is whitish meat clusters with small black seeds. Fruit can be eaten fresh, made into a drink or added to ice cream.

Star Apple, Caimite (Trinidad & Tobago) – small round milky fruit green or maroon in color inside and out. Fleshy, with small black seeds, stainy when not quite ripe. Taste almost like persimmons.

Whitey, Pois Doux (Trinidad & Tobago) – large, black seeds covered with sweet white heavy flesh, contained in a pod (10-12" long).

Mittai   Finger size pastry made from flour and water cut into thin strips, cooked and dripped into sugar mixture.

Money   **Old English Coins** - used in British Guiana.
Bit - silver six-sided coin worth eight cents.
Cent - copper coin, size of American penny, worth one cent.
Penny - larger copper coin worth two cents.
Shilling – round silver coin, size of American quarter, worth 24 cents.
Sixpence – round silver coin worth twelve cents, slightly larger than an American dime.

Pone   Dessert made with grated cassava, grated coconut, sugar, margarine, black pepper. Raisins are optional.

Proverbs   Wise sayings, some colloquial, passed down through generations, sometimes meaning is not readily understood.

Salara　　　　Rolled pastry log with stewed grated coconut dyed red between the dough, and sliced diagonally.

Stelling　　　Pier or wharf.

Stretcher　　　Stretch candy.

Tennis Roll　　Slightly sweet roll with smooth top, usually eaten with cheese.

Wheelwright　A person who makes or repairs wagon wheels.